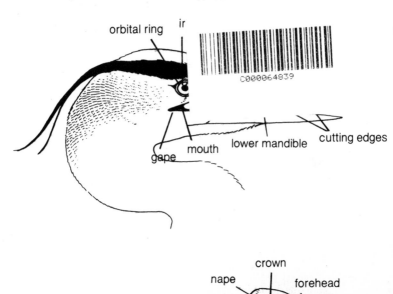

orbital ring
ir
gape
mouth
lower mandible
cutting edges

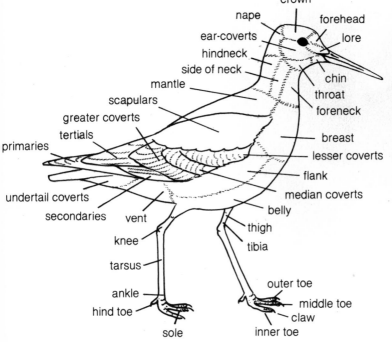

crown
nape
forehead
ear-coverts
lore
hindneck
side of neck
chin
mantle
throat
scapulars
foreneck
greater coverts
tertials
breast
primaries
lesser coverts
flank
undertail coverts
median coverts
secondaries
vent
belly
knee
thigh
tarsus
tibia
ankle
outer toe
hind toe
middle toe
claw
sole
inner toe

EX LIBRIS

to   Joan.   1982

Happy Xmas

me X

The RSPB Book of
British Birds

Peter Holden • JTR Sharrock
Illustrated by Hilary Burn

Macmillan London

The illustration of a bird's topography
was drawn by Alan Harris.

ISBN 0 333 34246 1

First published 1982 by
Macmillan London Limited
London and Basingstoke.

Associated companies in Auckland, Dallas,
Delhi, Dublin, Hong Kong, Johannesburg,
Lagos, Manzini, Melbourne, Nairobi,
New York, Singapore, Tokyo, Washington
and Zaria.

Composition by Filmtype Services Ltd., Scarborough.
Printed in Italy by New Interlitho, Milan.

Contents

Introduction

The aim of this book is to provide the beginner—young or old—with basic, reliable, interesting information on all the species of birds he or she is likely to see in the first couple of years of birdwatching in Britain and Ireland.

The RSPB Book of British Birds differs from many other bird books by covering only those species seen regularly in the British Isles. Although giving key points for the identification of 272 species, it is more than just a field guide, since it also contains background information on each species, from which the beginner can gain a deeper understanding of our bird life.

Hilary Burn's beautiful illustrations show all the species in characteristic positions and in the various plumages in which they are likely to be seen. The scenes illustrated have been carefully planned by the authors to show the habitats in which the birds are likely to be encountered; the pictures, therefore, contain additional information which will help beginners.

No experienced birdwatcher relies on sight alone when in the field. The songs and calls of birds are a valuable aid to identification, but difficult to describe, and although many are included in this book, the beginner should listen to the excellent sound recordings currently available.

A feature of this guide is the special two-page treatment given to six selected, well-known species. The additional information shows something of the fascination which can come from studying birds in the wild.

The sequence of the species in this book follows the scientific order recommended by Dr K. H. Voous. There are three good reasons for this arrangement: first, this is the 'natural' order, with closely related species near to each other. The novice birdwatcher will soon learn to place a new bird in its group or family (for example, a Redwing is a thrush, so it can be found near to the familiar Song Thrush in this list). Second, most bird books, journals and ornithological lists follow the same or a very similar order, and it is therefore helpful to become familiar with it as early as possible. Third, the alternative arrangement by habitats is inappropriate, as most birds are found outside their normal habitats from time to time.

No abbreviations appear in the text, so each section is easy to read. A few terms regularly used by birdwatchers have, however, been included and for readers to whom their meaning is unclear definitions have been provided either in the Glossary on page v or in the explanation of a bird's topography. In the illustrations, ♀ stands for female and ♂ for male.

Knowing the approximate size of a bird is vital if a correct identification is to be made. Estimation of size in the field is, however, very difficult. The conventional metric measurement is taken from tip of beak to tip of tail when the bird is laid flat on its back. This metric measurement is included in the identification section, but observers will probably find it more helpful to use the comparison in size with a familiar species, which precedes most measurements. It has been assumed, therefore, that observers will be familiar with a small number of very common birds.

Glossary of Terms

Brood   Young birds in nest (or just out of nest), all from one clutch

Camouflage, cryptic: blending with the background; *disruptive*: bold patterning which helps to disguise shape

Clutch   Eggs in nest all laid by one bird

Courtship   A bird's behaviour when attracting and keeping a mate

Crèche   A group of young ducks from different families which are still dependent on an adult, but not necessarily one of their own parents

Dabbling ducks   Species of ducks which usually feed on or near the water surface

Display   Visual signals given by a bird, often associated with courtship

Drumming   Instrumental noise. Woodpeckers use their bill to drum on wood. A Snipe's tail feathers make a bleating sound during display, which is called drumming

Eclipse   The camouflage plumage which is grown by ducks while moulting their flight feathers

Feral   Living wild, although released by man, or having escaped from captivity

Field mark   A plumage feature which aids identification (e.g. white wing-bars)

Genus   A scientific grouping of closely allied species which is indicated by the first word of the scientific name (e.g. all divers are in the genus *Gavia*)

Gizzard   Part of a bird's digestive system, where food is broken up

Gliding   Flying on a straight course with no wingbeats

Habitat   Area with distinct vegetation in which bird species (and other animal species) are also usually distinct

Immature   A bird which has left the nest but which is not yet in its fully adult plumage; depending on the species, it may be from a fledgling to four years old

Introduction   A bird deliberately released by man, now breeding wild

Invasion   An unusually large movement of birds into an area for a relatively short period

Irruption   Some species have an irregular one-way movement away from an area of high population or food shortage – this is known as an eruption. Their arrival in a new area is an irruption

Jizz   Characteristic postures, stance or actions of a bird which help identify it

Juvenile   A young bird which has left the nest but retains some of its first plumage

Migration   The movement from one area to another, followed, at a different season, by a return to the original area

Moult   The natural loss and replacement of feathers

Moult migration   Migration to and from a special area for the moult period

Nocturnal   Active at night

Passage migrant   A bird which passes through the British Isles on its migration

Pellet   A solid mass of indigestible food ejected through a bird's mouth rather than passed as droppings

Plumage   A bird's covering of feathers

Race   A subspecies

Raptor   Day-flying bird of prey—not owl

Resident   Bird which remains in the same area throughout the year

Roost   To rest or sleep; a gathering of birds at their communal sleeping place

Sawbill   A member of the merganser family. The name is derived from tooth-like projections along the edge of the bill which help the bird hold fish

Soaring   Circling, effortless flight, often in thermals

Species   Animal or plant of one sort (e.g. House Sparrow) which can produce a new generation identical to itself

Speculum   The coloured patch on a duck's wing

Subspecies   Subdivision of a species, the individuals of which all look similar (but different from those of other subspecies) and breed in a distinct geographical area

Territory   An area, usually (but not always) around a nest-site, which is defended by a bird or pair of birds from others of the same species

Thermal   Rising column of hot air caused by sun or land surface

Red-throated Diver *Gavia stellata*

This, the most common of Britain's divers, breeds on small, remote, upland lochs, where there are few fish, and regular flights are made by the parents to bring food for their young from lowland lochs, estuaries or the sea.

On their breeding grounds these divers are quite noisy. Calls include harsh, barking warning-calls and weird wails. They have exciting displays and fly over their territories calling, a habit once thought to predict rain!

Divers are easily disturbed while breeding and birdwatchers wanting to see Red-throats should look on larger lochs, where they fish, and avoid visiting breeding sites.

In autumn, these divers leave their Highland homes and winter on coastal waters, occasionally appearing inland, especially after gales. Often seen singly, but sometimes in small groups.

Black-throated Diver *Gavia arctica*

Like the previous species, the Black-throated Diver is a summer visitor to remote lochs in northern Scotland; it usually nests on islands in larger lochs. Those breeding are often disturbed by tourists, fishermen and birdwatchers; recently, fewer young have been reared, causing concern for the future of this very beautiful, but rare breeding species.

Black-throated Divers may stay underwater for as long as two minutes, but the average dive for fish lasts about 45 seconds.

Although silent for most of the year, a variety of calls may be heard in spring, including a drawn-out wail.

Great Northern Diver *Gavia immer*

Known as the Common Loon in North America, this large diver is sometimes seen around the coast of Scotland in summer, but nesting has only once been proved in Britain. The nearest breeding population is in Iceland.

Beautifully adapted to its aquatic life, this diver can slip underwater with barely a ripple, and when alarmed swims low in the water with only head and neck visible. To take off, it needs a long run along the surface of the water.

The White-billed Diver *Gavia adamsii* is sometimes seen in British waters, chiefly in winter. It is much rarer than the similar Great Northern, from which it is distinguished by its wholly pale and usually upswept bill.

Red-throated Diver
Size of Mallard – 60 cm. In breeding plumage (**1**) has dull red throat, grey head, dark back and white underparts. Grey and white in winter (**2**) with white around eye. Slender bill often tilted upwards. Hunch-backed and thin-necked in flight.
Breeds on small lochs in north and west Scotland. A few pairs nest in Ireland. Seen around the coast in winter, also visits inland lakes and reservoirs.

Black-throated Diver
Slightly larger than Mallard – 65 cm. Grey head, black throat bordered with white stripes, and white patches on back in summer (**3**). In winter (**4**) appears darker than Red-throat with dark cap to level of eye and pale thigh patch. Dagger-like bill held horizontal.
Breeds on large lochs in northwest Scotland. Seen in coastal waters in winter and sometimes on inland lakes.

Great Northern Diver
Larger than Mallard – 80 cm. Thick neck and heavy bill. In summer (**5**) has black head and neck with white collars; back is chequered black and white. In winter (**6**) has pale area around eye. Thick neck and relatively slow wingbeats aid identification in flight.
Seen around coast of Scotland in summer and more southern coasts in winter, rarely coming inland.

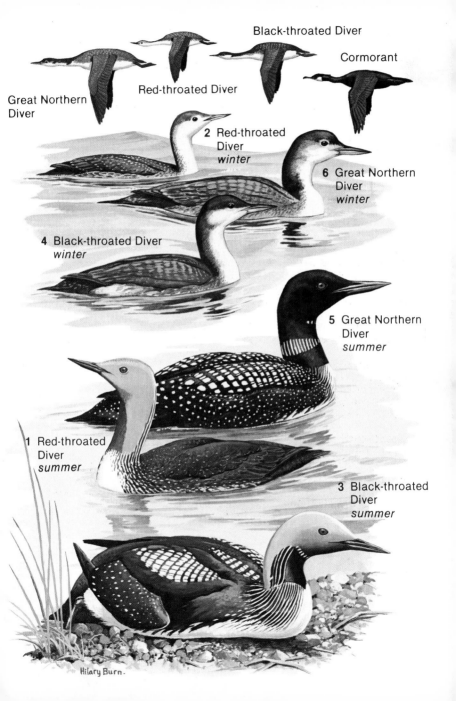

Black-throated Diver

Cormorant

Red-throated Diver

Great Northern
Diver

2 Red-throated
Diver
winter

6 Great Northern
Diver
winter

4 Black-throated Diver
winter

5 Great Northern
Diver
summer

1 Red-throated
Diver
summer

3 Black-throated
Diver
summer

Hilary Burn.

Great Crested Grebe *Podiceps cristatus*

With legs situated under its tail, the Great Crested Grebe is ungainly and rarely seen on land, but supreme under water. It feeds mainly on fish, which it chases below the surface, usually at a depth of 2–4 m, and regularly stays submerged for 26 seconds or more.

The ritual of this grebe's courtship has been much studied as it is beautiful, highly stylized and quite easily observed. A pair will display their crests and 'tippits' to each other by repeatedly shaking their heads. Sometimes both will dive, bring up weed and adopt an upright position while pressing their breasts together and shaking their heads from side to side.

The nest is usually a floating raft of vegetation, anchored to a branch or to aquatic plants. Both sexes incubate the eggs. When the adults leave the nest they generally cover the eggs with weed to conceal them from crows and other predators.

Young grebes frequently ride on the backs of their parents as this gives them protection from their main enemy, the pike. Adult grebes can frequently be seen feeding their young with feathers and will also eat feathers themselves; it is likely that this helps grebes to form pellets of the indigestible items – the fish bones being ejected wrapped up with feathers.

In the 19th century, the Great Crested Grebe was rare and was almost exterminated as a breeding species in Britain because its dense fur-like breast feathers were used for making muffs for Victorian ladies. Protection laws, the construction of gravel pits and reservoirs and, perhaps, a slight change in the climate have fortunately resulted in the species becoming more common again. In future, however, this grebe is likely to suffer from the increasing use of lakes for water sports which may reduce its breeding success in areas where it is most numerous.

Great Crested Grebe
Slightly smaller than Mallard – 48 cm. Long, slender, white neck; dagger-like bill; grey-brown back and blackish-crown and crest in winter (**1**). Chestnut frills around head when breeding (**2**). Dives frequently. Seldom seen in flight. Juveniles (**3**) have dark stripes on sides of neck. Most common call is growling 'gorr'. *Breeds on freshwater lakes, reservoirs, gravel pits and sometimes on rivers. Present in most parts of Britain, rarer in northern Scotland and southwest England. Often seen on the sea in winter, especially in estuaries.*

Great Crested Grebes

display

1 *winter*

3 *juvenile*

2 *summer*

Little Grebe *Tachybaptus ruficollis*

A loud trilling or 'whinnying' is a typical sound of summer around many ponds or lakes. The call tells us that a Little Grebe or Dabchick is not far away, but seeing it may be difficult.

Once a Little Grebe is disturbed, it slips underwater with hardly a ripple, and usually emerges again out of sight, often among nearby vegetation, or swims with just its head showing above the water.

Little Grebes are at home in a variety of habitats, from remote moorland tarns to town park ponds or even on the sea in winter. They prefer relatively shallow water, where they feed on insects, shellfish and small fish, which they catch up to 2 m below the surface.

Red-necked Grebe *Podiceps grisegena*

A winter visitor to Britain from Denmark and north-eastern Europe, arriving in small numbers in October and moving back in March. Usually seen on the sea, often in estuaries, but sometimes on inland waters.

In some winters, when the weather is particularly severe in northern Europe, many more Red-necked Grebes suddenly appear in British waters.

Slavonian Grebe *Podiceps auritus*

Like other members of this family, the Slavonian Grebe catches most of its prey underwater. The food includes small fish such as sticklebacks, and aquatic insects.

This species was first found nesting in the Scottish Highlands in 1908 and gradually increased to the 50 or so pairs which now nest annually. The number of young reared each year is often limited by changing water levels in breeding lochs, illegal egg-collecting and disturbance by holidaymakers, often birdwatchers.

Black-necked Grebe *Podiceps nigricollis*

Less often seen on the sea than Slavonian Grebes and may, in winter, even visit lakes and reservoirs in urban areas, where some show no fear of man.

Food usually consists of insects or their larvae, but small fish and shellfish are also eaten. Some food is taken from the surface of the water by skimming the bill from side to side. Other food is found by diving; dives usually last about 30 seconds.

Small, scattered breeding colonies of Black-necked Grebes are found in Europe, from Spain north to Denmark, but the species is most numerous in eastern Europe and the USSR.

Little Grebe
Smaller than Moorhen – 27 cm. Smallest grebe. Appears dumpy and blunt-tailed. In summer (**1**) has yellow base to bill, dark brown plumage with chestnut neck, throat and cheeks. Paler in winter (**2**) with dusky neck and face. *Widespread on lakes, quiet rivers and ponds.*

Red-necked Grebe
Smaller than Mallard – 45 cm. Chestnut neck, white cheeks, black crown to level of eye and yellow base to bill in summer (**3**). Grey and white in winter (**4**) with black crown to level of eye and dusky neck. *Winter visitor, mainly to east coast of England.*

Slavonian Grebe
Smaller than Mallard – 35 cm. In summer (**5**) has chestnut neck and flanks, black head and yellow tufts. In winter (**6**) is like Black-necked, but has flatter head, straight bill and whiter cheeks, contrasting with dark cap. *A winter visitor to coastal waters and inland lakes. A few nest in Scotland.*

Black-necked Grebe
Smaller than Mallard – 31 cm. Black head and neck, with gold feathers behind eye in summer (**7**). Bill often noticeably upturned. In winter (**8**) similar to Slavonian, but more rounded head and dark crown extending lower, especially behind eye, and merging with pale cheeks. *Rare breeding species. Winter visitor to coasts and inland lakes.*

Black-necked Grebe

Little Grebe

Slavonian Grebe

Red-necked Grebe

8 Black-necked Grebe *winter*

Great Crested Grebe

6 Slavonian Grebe *winter*

4 Red-necked Grebe *winter*

2 Little Grebe *winter*

5 Slavonian Grebe *summer*

3 Red-necked Grebe *summer*

7 Black-necked Grebe *summer*

1 Little Grebe *summer*

juvenile

Hilary Burn.

Fulmar *Fulmarus glacialis*

Wheeling Fulmars are now a common sight around most sea cliffs in Britain or Ireland, but this has not always been so. The numbers of Fulmars have undergone an amazing expansion during the last hundred years or so. Before 1878, the only British colony was on the remote island of St Kilda, 200 km from mainland Scotland, but since then they have spread right around our coasts. They may have been helped by the fishing industry because they feed on offal thrown from boats.

Fulmars do not breed until at least six years old and lay only one egg each year, but they have long lives, regularly reaching 17 years, and some are known to be over 30 years old.

Great Shearwater *Puffinus gravis*

Staring out to sea from a vantage point on the west coast of Britain or Ireland in August or September is the way one is most likely to see this master of flight.

Great Shearwaters are summer visitors to the Northern Hemisphere. They breed on a few remote islands in the South Atlantic and then migrate into the North Atlantic, moving first north and then west towards Europe. Often found near whales and porpoises.

Cory's Shearwaters *Calonectris diomedea* sometimes appear off our coast, especially from July to September. Brown above, merging to white below, and lacking dark cap.

Sooty Shearwater *Puffinus griseus*

Equally at home around the Antarctic pack ice or in the English Channel, the Sooty Shearwater is one of the world's greatest travellers. Its breeding colonies are on islands in the South Atlantic and Pacific Oceans and it visits the Northern Hemisphere between April and November. Searching the horizon through binoculars in rough weather is the way to find this species.

Manx Shearwater *Puffinus puffinus*

Vikings in long-boats heard the weird calls of Manx Shearwaters and included them among the 'evil spirits' of their sagas. On summer nights, those same sounds can still be heard as the birds approach their cliff-top colonies having spent the day feeding at sea. Shearwaters are clumsy and vulnerable on land, so darkness saves them from predators such as Great Black-backed Gulls. After nine weeks, the young are deserted by their parents and eight days later make their way down to the sea, where they start their long migration to a wintering area off the coast of South America.

Fulmar (1)
Smaller than Herring Gull – 47 cm. Gull-like, with stiff, straight wings. Shallow wingbeats and long glides. Thick neck and short, thick bill. Grey back, wing-tips and tail. Dark smudge around eye. White underparts.
Breeds in colonies on sea cliffs.

Great Shearwater (2)
Body shorter than Herring Gull – 47 cm, but longer wings. Large shearwater with brown back and white underparts; dark cap; white on tail. Strong wingbeats and long glides.
Seen mainly off western coasts, August–October.

Sooty Shearwater (3)
Smaller than Herring Gull – 46 cm. Torpedo-shaped body, long Swift-like wings and small head. Dark brown above and below except for white stripe on undersides of wings. Flies close to sea, often far out on horizon.
Seen off our coasts in August and September.

Manx Shearwater (4)
Smaller than Herring Gull – 34 cm. Black above, white below. Hurried, stiff wingbeats followed by glide over waves is typical, but also banks and glides. West Mediterranean race *P.p. mauretanicus* (5) is browner above and duskier below, some like Sooty without wing-stripe.
Mostly seen around western coasts especially in summer. Nests on islands. P.p. mauretanicus occurs June–October.

2 Great Shearwaters

3 Sooty Shearwaters

5 Manx Shearwater
P.p. mauretanicus

4 Manx Shearwaters

1 Fulmars

Hilary Burn

Storm Petrel *Hydrobates pelagicus*

This tiny seabird may sometimes be seen fluttering along behind a ship while searching for small fish, tiny sea creatures and even scraps thrown overboard.

Although active by day while at sea, it approaches land only after dark. The largest colonies are found on the remotest islands off northern and western Britain and Ireland. Some colonies, especially those in Ireland, number tens of thousands of pairs and their strange purring calls together with a strong musty smell make such nesting areas easy to locate. Nest-sites vary from holes in walls to burrows in the ground; some tunnels are dug by the petrel, others as side chambers to burrows already occupied by Puffins or even rabbits.

Leach's Petrel *Oceanodroma leucorhoa*

Gales in September are likely to bring these elusive seabirds to inshore waters, mainly on the western side of the British Isles. In some years, a few are found even on inland lakes and reservoirs.

Leach's Petrels visit their underground nest-sites only after dark and, because they prefer remote islands, only a few colonies have been found in Britain so far, although others may still await discovery.

Gannet *Sula bassana*

Nearly half the world's Gannet colonies are around the British Isles. Almost all of them are on cliffs or steep slopes of small isolated islands. Colonies are usually large: St Kilda, northwest of the Scottish mainland, has almost 60,000 pairs and is the largest 'gannetry' in the world.

When they first leave their nests, young Gannets cannot fly, but most start to swim southwards to the West African coast where they spend the winter. They may not return until their second or third summer. When they do return, they group around the edge of the breeding colonies, but do not nest until five or six years old. Gannets are long-lived, and often survive for 20 years or more if they do not get caught in fishing nets or die as a result of oil pollution or some other man-made accident.

Gannets plunge-diving for fish from 9 m or more are an exciting sight, hitting the water at 100 km per hour to catch fish at a depth of 12–15 m.

Storm Petrel (1)
Sparrow-sized – 16 cm. Black with white rump, rather like House Martin with square tail. Pale, often white, stripe on underwing. Weak fluttering flight near water, often patters surface with feet.
Most seen in summer. Nests on remote islands in north and west Britain and Ireland. Sometimes follows boats.

Leach's Petrel (2)
Larger than sparrow – 20 cm. Brownish-black with white rump which, at very close range, shows a dark line down the middle. Longer, more pointed wings than those of Storm. Tail is forked. Pale stripe on upperwings. May bank, glide and sometimes hover.
Nests on a few remote islands. Seen mainly in summer.

Gannet
Larger than any gull – 95 cm, long, narrow wings almost 2 m across. Pointed tail. Adults (3) are white with black wing-tips and yellow on back of head. Juveniles (4) vary from slate-grey on leaving nest, to white with black marks in their 2nd, 3rd or 4th years (5). Often glides close to waves, also seen in wheeling flocks. Feeds by plunge-diving into water.
Found in the open ocean at all times of year. Breeds on islands and rocky cliffs.

Gannets

adults

4 *juvenile*

juvenile

2 Leach's
Petrels

5 4th-year

1 Storm Petrels

3 Gannet
adult

Hilary Burn

Cormorant *Phalacrocorax carbo*

A Cormorant standing on a rock or breakwater with wings out-stretched is a familiar sight anywhere around our coasts. The reason for this behaviour is, however, disputed: is it drying its wings after a fishing expedition, or is this a relaxed position in which to digest fish? Ornithologists are uncertain.

Cormorants feed on fish – especially flat-fish, such as flounders, that live on the sea bed – which they catch by diving underwater for between 15 and 60 seconds in areas of relatively shallow water. Unfortunately, many Cormorants have been persecuted to preserve fish, which can hardly be justified as very few fish which they eat are of value to fishermen.

These birds are often seen in loose flocks, usually when moving between feeding and roosting areas. Where Cormorants are common, groups can often be seen standing around, sitting in trees, or even perched on pylons.

In Britain, Cormorants nest on cliff ledges usually near the sea and the only territory which they defend is immediately around the nest, although in some colonies conditions are so cramped that nests are actually touching. In parts of Europe, Cormorants nest inland in trees and these trees are sometimes killed by the Cormorants' droppings.

Shag *Phalacrocorax aristotelis*

Around the British Isles, Shags outnumber Cormorants by almost ten to one, and in some places their numbers continue to increase.

Although similar in appearance to Cormorants, Shags fill a separate niche in the ecology of our coasts and the two species do not really compete for food: Shags prefer free-swimming fish and generally hunt in deeper water. Prey is often caught by diving from a swimming position although they will, like Cormorants, sometimes spring out of the water as they dive. A favourite food is sandeels.

Shags can be found around rocky coasts throughout the year, but only after particularly severe gales are they seen on inland waters. Although not truly migratory, some – especially from colonies in the west – do make their way southwards to French or even Spanish waters.

Cormorant
Heron-sized – 90 cm. Large, blackish with long thick neck and heavy bill. Throat and part of cheeks white. Breeding adults (**1**) have shaggy crest on back of head and white thigh patch which are lost in winter (**2**). Juvenile and 1st-winter birds (**3**) are brown, often with pale neck and belly. Stands upright or swims, often with head and bill up-tilted like Red-throated Diver. *In summer, is found on rocky coasts, mainly in the west, and always near shallow bays. In winter, is also seen inland on lakes and rivers.*

Shag
Smaller than Cormorant – 75 cm. Finer bill and thinner neck than Cormorant. In flight, notice smaller head and faster wingbeats. Iridescent green feathers of adult (**4**) usually appear blackish. Crest only in spring, when breeding starts. Base of bill yellow. Adults in winter (**5**) are more brown, with pale chin and throat. Juveniles (**6**) are brown, less white on belly than young Cormorants, but have white patch on chin. *Found along rocky coasts and islands. Rarely seen inland.*

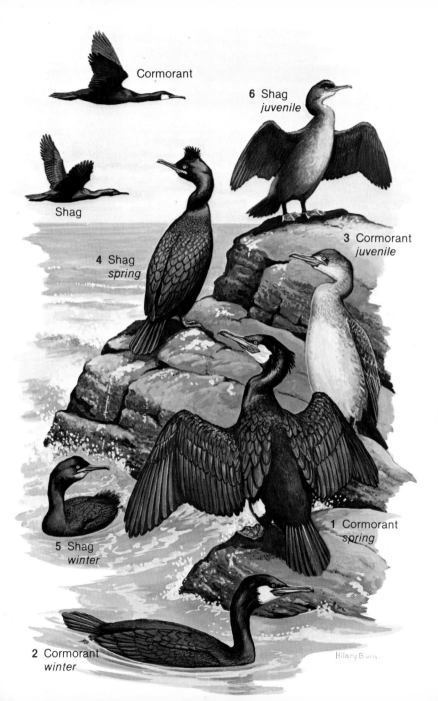

Cormorant

6 Shag *juvenile*

Shag

4 Shag *spring*

3 Cormorant *juvenile*

5 Shag *winter*

1 Cormorant *spring*

2 Cormorant *winter*

Hilary Burn

Bittern *Botaurus stellaris*

Large reedbeds are the home of this rare and secretive bird. By 1868, Bitterns had ceased to breed in Britain because many wetlands had been drained, they were hunted as food and, as they became rarer, collectors shot them to preserve their skins and took their eggs. Fortunately, they recolonised early this century and now nest in a few British reedbeds again.

Although fish are the chief food, amphibians, insects, worms, small mammals and even young birds are also eaten. The spring call is a famous 'boom' similar to someone blowing across the top of an empty bottle.

Bitterns have cryptic camouflage and blend with reeds. When alarmed, they stretch their neck, point their bill upwards and sway like reeds in the wind.

In winter, European Bitterns reach Britain and it is then that they visit more open, but still marshy habitats. In severe winters, many of these wandering birds fail to find sufficient food and die.

Grey Heron *Ardea cinerea*

Unless you have seen a heronry, you may find it hard to believe that these birds are at home in trees, only rarely nesting on the ground or on cliff ledges.

Herons may lay eggs as early as February. Eleven weeks later, young Herons are trying out their wings and clambering around the heronry. After leaving the nest, the young often wander far from the colony – a way of ensuring they do not compete for food.

Herons often stand motionless in slow-moving water, neck stretched forward, waiting to strike at a passing fish. But not only fish are eaten: the diet includes amphibians, small mammals, insects, worms and birds. When not feeding, Herons often roost at traditional 'standing grounds' where sometimes several will gather.

Although northern European Grey Herons are long-distance migrants, ours seldom leave the British Isles; in severe winters, many do not find enough food, and die.

The rare Purple Heron *Ardea purpurea* is smaller, more slender and is tinged rufous; a few occur as vagrants from May to September.

Spoonbill *Platalea leucorodia*

Long ago Spoonbills nested in England, but now they are unusual summer visitors from colonies in Holland. Their curiously shaped bills are swept from side to side in shallow water in their search for prey, mainly fish or insects.

Bittern (1)
Smaller than Grey Heron – 75 cm. Golden brown with darker marks. Black 'moustache' and crown. Dagger-like bill. Neck often withdrawn, but can appear long and thin. In flight, head is drawn back onto shoulders and wings are broad and rounded.
Very secretive. Nests in dense reedbeds. In winter, may visit open marshy areas.

Grey Heron
Very large – 94 cm. Adult (2) has grey back, white underparts, long thin white neck with black marks. Wispy crest, long legs. Often stands hunched up on one leg. Flies with head drawn back, large broad wings and trailing legs. Juvenile and 1st-winter (3) have smaller crest, dark crown and darker neck. Usual call is loud, harsh 'frank'.
Nests in trees in most parts of Britain and Ireland. Feeds by water but sometimes stands in fields and other dry areas.

Spoonbill
Smaller than Grey Heron – 85 cm. Graceful, long-necked white bird with long legs and long 'spoon-shaped' bill. Adult in breeding plumage (4) has crest and yellow breast band. Juvenile (5) has pink bill and black wing-tips.
Rare visitor to eastern and southern Britain. Mainly marshes near the coast and estuaries.

heronry

5 Spoonbill *juvenile*

Grey Heron

1 Bittern

3 Grey Heron *juvenile*

2 Grey Heron

4 Spoonbill

Mute Swan *Cygnus olor*

The Mute Swan, one of the world's heaviest birds, is as much at home on a town park pond as on a remote Irish loch. The long neck helps the bird to reach underwater plants and, if it 'up-ends', it can reach up to a metre below the surface.

Swan meat was once considered a delicacy and swans were semi-domesticated. To prove ownership some bills were marked – a tradition still carried out on the River Thames in the famous 'swan upping' ceremony.

The Mute Swan is not totally silent: it has a variety of calls, especially snorts or hisses when defending a territory. In flight the wings make a rhythmic whistling.

Downy young are regularly carried on their parents' backs which keeps them warm and protects them from predators such as pike. Males are often seen with wings raised and head back when driving off an intruder.

Bewick's Swan *Cygnus columbianus*

Named after the 18th century engraver Thomas Bewick, who was responsible for many bird portraits, this is the smallest swan to visit the British Isles.

The pattern on the bill differs from bird to bird and individuals can be identified. We now know that pairs stay together for years and 'divorce' is rare. If one of a pair dies, the other may take up to three years to find a new mate.

On their breeding grounds in Arctic Russia, young Bewick's Swans mature very quickly (much faster than Whoopers or Mutes) which enables them to take advantage of short Arctic summers. Family groups migrate together, spend the winter together and even leave together, although they summer separately.

Whooper Swan *Cygnus cygnus*

In autumn about three-quarters of the Whooper Swans in Iceland migrate to the British Isles. During the breeding season the swans live on lakes and streams, rich in iron-compounds which stain the head and neck of many of them. This colouring is lost during the winter when old feathers are moulted.

Whooper Swans also breed in Scandinavia and northern Russia, but it is likely that only a few from these areas ever reach the British Isles. Some Whoopers summer in Scotland and occasionally breed successfully.

Swans fly high when migrating. A flock of 30 swans, probably Whoopers, were seen by a pilot flying at a height of 8,000 m.

Mute Swan
Very large – 150 cm. Long thin neck with graceful curve. Adults are white with orange-and-black bill: the male or cob (**1**) has larger black knob on bill than the female or pen (**2**). Juveniles or cygnets (**3**) are brown with pale bills. *Found on fresh water almost everywhere in Britain and Ireland. Occasionally on the sea.*

Bewick's Swan
Smaller than Mute – 120 cm. Adult (**4**) is all white with relatively short straight neck and domed head. Bill is black with yellow base forming variable pattern, but yellow mark generally rounded, not wedge-shaped. Often makes a musical honking, especially when in flocks. Juvenile (**5**) is grey with black-and-pinkish bill. *Winter visitor to inland lakes in southern Britain and Ireland.*

Whooper Swan
Size of Mute Swan – 150 cm. Adult (**6**) all white with wedge-shaped yellow patch on black bill. Straight neck with base often resting on back giving 'kinked' effect. Larger bill than Bewick's. Some adults (**7**) have rust-coloured staining on neck. Juvenile (**8**) is brown with pink-and-black bill. Loud trumpeting call. *Winter visitor mainly to northern Britain and Ireland with a few remaining in Scotland in summer.*

Bewick's Swan

Whooper Swan

Mute Swan

5 Bewick's Swan *juvenile*

7 Whooper Swan *stained*

Mute Swan

3 Mute Swan *juvenile*

8 Whooper Swan *juvenile*

6 Whooper Swan

4 Bewick's Swan

2 Mute Swan ♀

1 Mute Swan ♂

Hilary Burn.

Bean Goose *Anser fabalis*

Breeds in northern Europe and the USSR. Within the vast area inhabited by this species, different forms have evolved (called subspecies or races), and some even nest in dense forests. In winter, Bean Geese migrate to various parts of Europe, but only a few reach Britain.

Pink-footed Goose *Anser brachyrhynchus*

The evening flight of Pink-feet from their farmland feeding grounds to the safety of a nearby estuary or lake is one of the most spectacular winter sights.

The Pink-feet which migrate to the British Isles in late September breed in Iceland or even Greenland. Greater numbers used to visit England, but the increase in barley-growing in Scotland has provided better winter feeding and now the geese do not need to move so far south. The birds graze grass and growing shoots, including cereals and other crops. Although there is some conflict with farming interests, these geese do comparatively little damage.

White-fronted Goose *Anser albifrons*

Two separate races of White-fronts visit the British Isles in winter. One, from the USSR, migrates into Europe and reaches England or Wales, especially around Slimbridge on the Severn Estuary; the other race, from Greenland, winters mainly in Scotland and Ireland.

Geese migrate in family groups, and juvenile White-fronts stay with their parents during their first winter.

In some areas, these geese have moved from traditional wet meadows or bogs onto farmland, although the main food remains grasses. Research has shown that White-fronts are able to select the most nutritious grasses from a field.

Greylag Goose *Anser anser*

Once, this goose nested in the fenland of East Anglia. The name Greylag is probably derived from the fact that this was the grey goose which lagged behind the others: the one which lingered in spring, with some remaining to breed. Now, due to drainage and changes in agriculture, our only native breeding population is in northern Scotland, especially the Outer Hebrides, although feral Greylags breed in other areas.

The large bill of the Greylag is used, not only for grazing grasses, but also for digging up and eating roots or cutting through tough vegetation. In winter, Greylags from Iceland reach Britain, where they feed on farmland by day and roost on pools, lakes or estuaries.

Bean Goose (1)
Larger than Pink-foot – 68–84 cm. Dark brown plumage with orange legs. Head and neck very dark, almost black on forehead. Large bill with variable pattern. In flight, head appears long and neck is longer and darker than on other 'grey geese'. *Scarce winter visitor to farmland.*

Pink-footed Goose (2)
Smaller than Bean – 60–75 cm. Pinkish-brown plumage and pink legs. Bill has variable pink-and-black pattern. Short dark neck, short bill and rounded head are obvious in flight, as are pale grey forewings. *Winter visitor to Scotland and parts of England near coasts.*

White-fronted Goose
Larger than Pink-foot – 65–78 cm. Adult (3) has greyish-brown plumage and wide, white surround to pink or orange bill. Legs are orange. Black bars and blotches on belly. Relatively short neck and long wings in flight. Juvenile (4) lacks white on face and bars on belly. *Winter visitor to low-lying grassland.*

Greylag Goose (5)
Large grey-brown goose – 75–90 cm. Large pale head, thick pale neck, heavy orange bill, pink legs. Orange ring around eye. Broad wings with large bluish-grey patches. *Wild Greylags nest in north and west Scotland, others visit in winter. Feral Greylags now breed in many parts of Britain.*

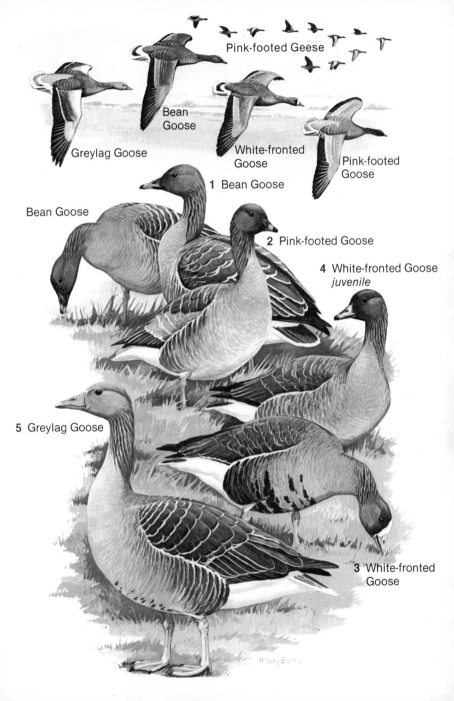

Pink-footed Geese

Bean Goose

Greylag Goose

White-fronted Goose

Pink-footed Goose

Bean Goose

1 Bean Goose

2 Pink-footed Goose

4 White-fronted Goose *juvenile*

5 Greylag Goose

3 White-fronted Goose

Hilary Burn

Canada Goose *Branta canadensis*

Introduced from North America in the reign of Charles II, since when it has become a popular bird in parks, and also nests wild in many areas. In some places, it has become so numerous that it is considered a nuisance because of the damage it does to crops.

During their annual moult, geese become flightless. Many Canada Geese in North America migrate to traditional areas where they can moult safely. Now, in Britain, some English Canadas make a regular moult migration to the Beauly Firth in northern Scotland.

In North America, there may be more than 15 different races of Canada Geese, varying considerably in size and colour. Some Canadas fly to Greenland to moult, and there they sometimes mix with flocks of Barnacle Geese and occasionally migrate with them to Britain; so there are genuine records of wild Canada Geese in Britain as well as the feral ones.

Barnacle Goose *Branta leucopsis*

Those Barnacles which migrate to Britain for the winter come from either Spitsbergen or Greenland. Spitsbergen birds visit the Solway Firth and those from Greenland fly to western Scotland or Ireland. The two populations do not mix, but both have increased in recent years.

Like the other geese, a Barnacle is white above and below the tail, which is a visual signal and helps to keep birds together, especially when flying in 'V' formation or in diagonal lines.

Back on their breeding grounds, these geese often nest on inaccessible cliff-faces, which gives them protection from predators such as Arctic foxes.

Brent Goose *Branta bernicla*

The High Arctic tundra is where Brent Geese breed. Dark-bellied Brents breed in Siberia; the light-bellied race comes to us from Spitsbergen, Greenland and northern Canada. Food is plentiful in the Arctic, but the summer is short: nesting starts before the snow and ice melt and the geese must leave within 100 days. In bad summers, hardly any young are reared.

In the 1930s, numbers of Brent Geese fell dramatically following disease in their chief winter food, eel-grass, which grows on mud-flats.

Protection, a succession of good breeding summers and the recovery of the eel-grass have resulted in a remarkable improvement. Even more surprising is the recent change in the habits of the geese, which now often graze on farmland.

Canada Goose (1)

Largest goose – 95 cm. Black head with white patches, long black neck, brown body, pale breast. Call is a noisy, trumpet-like honking.
Found near lakes, reservoirs and park ponds. Widespread in England and parts of Wales, but scarce in Scotland and Ireland.

Barnacle Goose (2)

Smaller than Canada – 58–70 cm. White face. Crown, back of head, neck and breast are black. Grey back and pale underparts. Appears black-and-white in flight.
Winter visitor to western coasts of Scotland and Ireland.

Brent Goose

Size of Mallard – 56–61 cm. Small goose with short neck and small head. Dark back. Black head and neck, with white patches on neck of adult. Dark-bellied race (3) has very dark grey underparts; pale-bellied race (4) has much lighter underparts. Fast and manoeuvrable in flight. Juveniles (5) of both races lack white patches on necks and have pale wing-bars.
Winter visitor to coastal areas: dark-bellied in southern and eastern England; pale-bellied in Ireland and Northumberland.

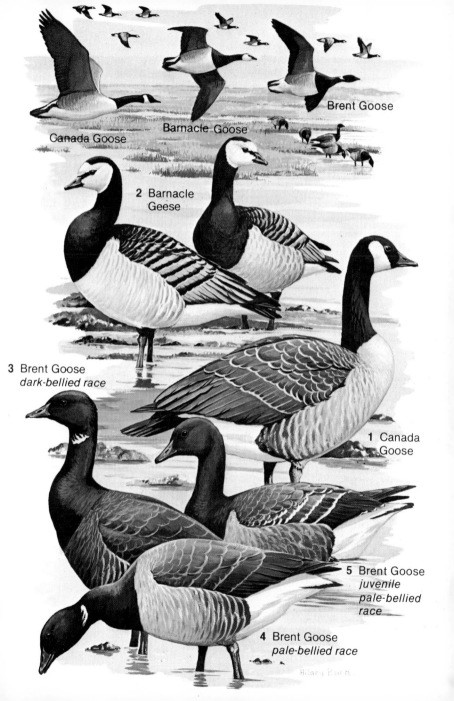

Canada Goose

Barnacle Goose

Brent Goose

2 Barnacle
Geese

3 Brent Goose
dark-bellied race

1 Canada
Goose

5 Brent Goose
*juvenile
pale-bellied
race*

4 Brent Goose
pale-bellied race

Hilary Burn

Egyptian Goose *Alopochen aegyptiacus*

More closely related to the Shelduck than to the geese. Egyptian Geese are native not only to Egypt, but to most of Africa, especially the sub-tropics, where they may nest at any time of year, especially the rainy season. The bird has escaped from wildfowl collections or been introduced to several parts of Britain. The largest population, numbering a few hundred, is to be found around lakes and rivers in Norfolk.

Shelduck *Tadorna tadorna*

Found all around our coast, except where the cliffs are steepest, but even there some will probably be found nearby in a tidal inlet or estuary.

Ducks' bills have tooth-like projections called lamellae along each side, which the Shelduck uses when filtering wet sand or mud during its search for *Hydrobia ulvea*, a small snail which is its most important food.

Shelducks nest in many different sites: under buildings, in trees, on stacks of straw and, most common of all, in rabbit burrows in old sand dunes. Newly hatched young travel with their parents to suitable feeding areas, but after about a week the family often splits up and the young band together in crèches of as many as 100 or more, with only a few adults in attendance. The young later become more independent, and may even brood one another.

In about July, adults start to leave their breeding grounds and fly to traditional moulting areas. Many European Shelducks gather off the coast of Holland and West Germany, but others moult in Bridgwater Bay in Somerset and in other estuaries. After moulting, they return to their breeding areas.

Mandarin *Aix galericulata*

This attractive duck was, as its name suggests, first brought from China or Japan as an ornamental species for parks and gardens. During this century escapes started to breed and feral populations have become established.

Mandarins are very secretive and are usually found on lakes fringed with trees and shrubs which overhang the water. They are more at home in woodland than are our other ducks; in flight they can easily manoeuvre between trees, and regularly perch on branches. Mandarins usually use holes in trees as nest-sites.

Outside the breeding season, in places where Mandarins are common, they may be seen in flocks.

Egyptian Goose
Larger than Shelduck – 68 cm. Unlike either typical duck or goose. Has long legs and upright stance. Heavy bill. Adult (**1**) has brown smudge around eye, dark collar, brown patch on breast and green speculum. Back is either red-brown or grey. Large white wing-patches in flight. Young in their 1st winter (**2**) are duller, without eye-patch and breast spot.
Found near inland lakes in East Anglia.

Shelduck
Larger than Mallard – 62 cm. Adult is white with red bill and legs, dark green head, and brown breast band. Black wing-tips obvious in flight. Green speculum. Male (**3**) has knob on bill. Female (**4**) has less well defined pattern and narrower breast band. Juvenile (**5**) is grey-brown above with white face.
Found in coastal areas, especially estuaries. Will visit inland lakes and sometimes nests inland.

Mandarin
Smaller than Mallard – 45 cm. Adult male (**6**) is very striking with crest, broad white eye-stripe, multi-coloured plumage, red bill, long orange neck feathers and orange 'sails'. Female (**7**) has grey-brown upperparts, spotted flanks and white 'spectacles'. Male in eclipse resembles female. Whistling call. In flight, both sexes show white belly and green speculum.
Around wood-fringed lakes in a few parts of Britain.

Mandarins

Shelduck

Egyptian Goose

1 Egyptian Geese

2 Egyptian Goose *juvenile*

5 Shelduck *juvenile*

7 Mandarin ♀

3 Shelduck ♂

6 Mandarin ♂

4 Shelduck ♀

Hilary Burn

Mallard *Anas platyrhynchos*

The most widespread duck in the world: found throughout the Northern Hemisphere and has been introduced to Australia and New Zealand. It has been domesticated for over 2,000 years and there are now many breeds which are kept for eggs or for eating.

The Mallard is one of several duck species which find much of their food on or near the surface of the water and are known as 'dabbling ducks'. The Mallard's food is varied and includes seeds and other vegetable matter, insects and their larvae, small shellfish and even frogs. To find their food, they will often 'up-end' and occasionally dive; more often, they will fly to nearby fields to feed after dark.

Like other ducks, the male, or drake, is more colourful than the female, or duck. The drake's bright plumage is used in courtship, but he plays no part in nest-building, incubation or rearing the young. The duck is cryptically camouflaged with her mottled plumage and dark line disguising her eye. The nest is made from grass, leaves and down, plucked from the duck's own breast. Although usually situated on the ground, the nest may be in a tree, 10 m or more from the ground.

Young Mallards leave the nest within 24 hours of hatching and can swim and feed themselves straightaway. If danger threatens, the duck will make a noisy getaway and the young will scatter and dive; with luck, the family will join up again when the danger is past.

Feathers must remain in good condition and all birds must moult and grow new feathers at least once a year. Mallards, like other ducks, moult at the end of their breeding season and drakes grow a drab camouflage-plumage and resemble the ducks; they are then said to be 'in eclipse'. For about two weeks they are flightless, but after their flight-feathers are regrown they gradually moult their body feathers again and the drakes reappear in their breeding plumage.

Most Mallards are resident in the British Isles, but in winter they are joined by others from Iceland or northern Europe.

Mallard
50–65 cm. Male (**1**) has bottle-green head, white collar, purple-brown breast, grey body and black tail with two curly feathers. Purple speculum. Female (**2**) is mottled brown with purple speculum and dark stripe through eye. Males in eclipse (**3**) (June–September) resemble females but have yellow bills and darker crowns. Call of female is familiar 'kwark-kwark'; male's call is quieter 'arrk'. *Common throughout Britain and Ireland on ponds, lakes, reservoirs, rivers and coastal marshes. Often seen on the sea in winter.*

Mallards

♂ up-ending

juvenile

3 ♂ in eclipse

2 ♀

1 ♂

Hilary Burn.

Wigeon *Anas penelope*

Only small numbers of Wigeons breed in Britain; the flocks which appear in winter are mainly migrants from Iceland, northern Europe or even the USSR.

Once, Wigeons were seen regularly only on salt marshes and estuaries, but, following disease in an important food, eel-grass, in 1930, they started to range wider and are now frequent visitors to inland lakes, flood meadows and marshes.

The Wigeon is vegetarian and may often be seen grazing on grass, and picking up food from the water's edge or from the surface of a lake. Sometimes, it follows swans and picks up food which has been pulled out of deeper water and would normally be out of reach for a Wigeon. This is known as 'commensal feeding', one species benefiting another.

Teal *Anas crecca*

The Teal is the smallest European duck. In flight, a flock can resemble waders as they twist and turn with rapidly beating wings.

Teals may breed near fresh water in many localities, but it is the rushy moorland pools of northern Britain and Ireland where breeding numbers are greatest.

In winter, Teals from Iceland, Scandinavia and the USSR migrate to the British Isles. Largest numbers are seen around our coast, but many come inland where they feed in shallow water using their bills to filter mud in their search for seeds. Most feeding takes place at night, when there are fewer predators around. During the day, Teals can be seen roosting on water, often close together in small groups.

Garganey *Anas querquedula*

The Garganey is the only duck which migrates to Europe for the summer. In autumn, it returns to its winter quarters in West Africa. On its 5,000 km journey, it will cross the Mediterranean, the North African coast and the Sahara in a single flight. Some travel south through Spain, but return, the following spring, through Italy: this is known as loop migration.

The largest populations of Garganeys are in eastern Europe and the USSR; Britain is on the edge of the species range. Most of the small number which breed are found in southeastern England. The draining of many suitable breeding sites is one reason for the recent decline in the number breeding, but a change in climate may also have had an effect.

Wigeon
Smaller than Mallard – 48 cm. Small bill and rounded crown. Male (**1**) has chestnut head with buff stripe, grey body and pale breast. In flight, has white belly and shoulder patches. Call is far-carrying whistle, 'whee-oo'. Female (**2**) has dark green speculum. 1st-winter male is like adult without white shoulders. Commonly seen in flocks.
Breeds mainly in the north. Winter visitor to variety of wetlands farther south, particularly coastal marshes.

Teal
Much smaller than Mallard – 36 cm. Small short-necked duck. Male's (**3**) chestnut-and-green head often appears dark. Grey body, white stripe above wing and yellow patch near tail. Female (**4**) like small Mallard with green speculum. Rapid wing-beats, pale belly and white stripe on wings in flight. Piping call.
Breeds near reed-fringed lakes mainly in the north. Widespread in winter, liking shallow lakes, flooded fields and coastal marshes.

Garganey
Smaller than Mallard, slightly larger than Teal – 39 cm. Male (**5**) has white stripe over eye and, in flight, blue-grey forewing. Female (**6**) like Teal, but dark eye-stripe, pale stripe over eye and, in flight, grey forewing with duller speculum.
Summer visitor, March to September. Likes shallow, reedy pools.

Garganeys

Teals

Wigeons

5 Garganey ♂

4 Teal ♀

3 Teal ♂

6 Garganey ♀

Wigeon *juvenile*

2 Wigeon ♀

1 Wigeon ♂

Hilary Burn

Gadwall *Anas strepera*

The Gadwall was introduced into Britain around 1850 and is now established as a regular breeding species. The Brecklands of East Anglia were the original stronghold, but further areas have now been colonised. In winter, others arrive in Britain, many of them coming from Iceland.

The food of the Gadwall is mainly plants or seeds which are picked up from the water-surface, or obtained by 'up-ending' and reaching 30 cm or so below the surface. Sometimes Gadwalls follow species which feed in deeper water, such as Coots, Goldeneyes or Mute Swans, in order to pick up any food which floats to the top of the water.

Pintail *Anas acuta*

This very attractive duck is a rare breeding species in Britain and Ireland, but it is far more numerous in winter, when others fly in from Iceland, northern Europe and the northern USSR.

A variety of animal and vegetable food is picked from the surface water or taken when the birds 'up-end' to reach the bottom of deeper water. The long neck enables the Pintail to find food out of the reach of other 'dabbling ducks'. Male Pintails have slightly longer necks than do the females, which enables them to feed in even deeper water.

Shoveler *Anas clypeata*

Inside the long, broad bill of the Shoveler are rows of tiny spines called lamellae which are a most efficient filter for trapping the minute animals and plant remains which make up its diet. Although some food may occasionally be found by diving or by 'up-ending', the most usual method is for the bill to be used for filtering the surface water. Groups of Shovelers may feed close together and sometimes swim in circles or in lines, which stirs up the water and brings more food to the surface.

By October, most of the Shovelers which breed in the British Isles have moved south to France, Spain or Italy, while a few may reach the North African coast. They are replaced on our lakes, however, by others which migrate here from northern Europe and the USSR.

In areas where Shovelers breed, the males can often be seen chasing each other and displaying with a comical head-bobbing. Often these displays are accompanied by sharp 'took, took-took' calls.

Gadwall
Smaller than Mallard – 51 cm. Male (**1**) is grey with black tail and white speculum. Female (**2**) resembles female Mallard, but has white speculum, orange sides to bill and brown tail. Both sexes show white bellies in flight. Male has croaking call; female, soft 'quack'. In eclipse, male is like dark female.
Breeds mainly in East Anglia, around freshwater lakes. Visits inland lakes in other areas in winter.

Pintail
Mallard-size – 56–66 cm. Graceful, long-necked duck. Male (**3**) has 10 cm long pointed tail, white breast, brown head with white stripe and grey body. Female (**4**) is like female Mallard, but has longer neck, greyer plumage and grey bill. Long neck and tail obvious in flight. Male in eclipse is like grey female.
Mainly a winter visitor to estuaries or inland lakes. A few pairs breed, near shallow water.

Shoveler
Smaller than Mallard – 48 cm. Male (**5**) has green head, huge bill and white body with chestnut flanks and belly. Female (**6**) like female Mallard, but with large bill. In flight, wings appear set far back on body and both sexes show blue-grey patch on forewings: male brighter than female. In eclipse, male is similar to female. *In summer, likes shallow marshy areas. Widespread in winter.*

Shovelers

Mallard

Pintails

Gadwalls

Mallard ♀

2 Gadwall ♀

1 Gadwall ♂

6 Shoveler ♀

Shoveler ♂ *in partial eclipse*

5 Shoveler ♂

4 Pintail ♀

3 Pintail ♂

Hilary Burn

Red-crested Pochard *Netta rufina*

Small numbers of this attractive diving duck breed in Europe; others are winter migrants from the USSR.

Red-crested Pochards are common in collections of waterfowl and many have been introduced to ornamental lakes. In autumn, a few truly wild ones reach Britain but are usually impossible to distinguish from free-flying escapes.

Pochard *Aythya ferina*

This duck has become more common in recent years and appears to have benefited from gravel-pits, reservoirs and other man-made lakes.

Pochards eat mostly plants which grow below the surface of the water, especially a group known as stoneworts (*Chara*). They usually dive for about 15 seconds and feed at a depth of about 3 m. Males tend to dive in deeper water than females.

Like other diving ducks, Pochards are seldom seen alone outside of the breeding season and often large flocks can be seen on lakes where food is plentiful.

The Ferruginous Duck *Aythya nyroca* is a rare winter visitor from eastern Europe. Its chestnut plumage, white patch under the tail and domed head help to single it out from all other wildfowl, except some warm-coloured female Tufted Ducks with white under their tails.

Tufted Duck *Aythya fuligula*

Watch a family of Tufted Ducks and you will notice the young chasing midges or looking for seeds on the water surface, but sometimes diving to find midge larvae underwater. The adults dive deeper, as they feed mainly on molluscs, at a depth of 7 m or more.

In some areas, Tufted Ducks nest among colonies of gulls, which helps give protection to the sitting female; such nests are often more productive than those under bushes or among tussocks of grass.

Tufted Ducks are with us throughout the year, but many migrate here for the winter from Iceland, Scandinavia and northeast Europe. Some visit lakes in towns.

Scaup *Aythya marila*

This species has occasionally nested in Britain, but never regularly. The vast flocks which visit some of our estuaries are made up of winter migrants from Iceland or northern Europe. The chief food is shellfish; some flocks winter where sewage outlets flow into the sea and large mussel-beds have developed.

Red-crested Pochard
Size of Mallard – 55 cm. Male (1) has large orange head, red bill, black neck and belly, and white flanks. Female (2) is brown with pale cheeks and dark crown, grey bill with pink edges. White wing-bar shows in flight.
Introduced into parks. A few wild individuals visit eastern Britain in winter.

Pochard
Smaller than Mallard – 45 cm. Short neck and steep forehead. Male (3) has grey back, black breast and reddish-brown head. Female (4) is grey-brown with blotchy cheeks.
Found on freshwater lakes in winter. Breeds in small numbers, but scarce in Ireland.

Tufted Duck
Smaller than Mallard – 43 cm. Male (5) is black with white flanks and belly, and drooping crest on back of head. Female (6) is dark brown with pale brown flanks. Male in eclipse resembles female. Both male and female show white wing-bar in flight.
Breeds and winters on inland lakes or slow-flowing rivers.

Scaup
Smaller than Mallard – 47 cm. Male (7) has black head, breast and tail, white flanks, and grey back. Female (8) is dark brown with large white patch at base of bill; (beware: female Tufted Duck has similar white patch). Both sexes have broad white wing-bar and bluish bill.
Winter visitor to coastal waters, especially estuaries.

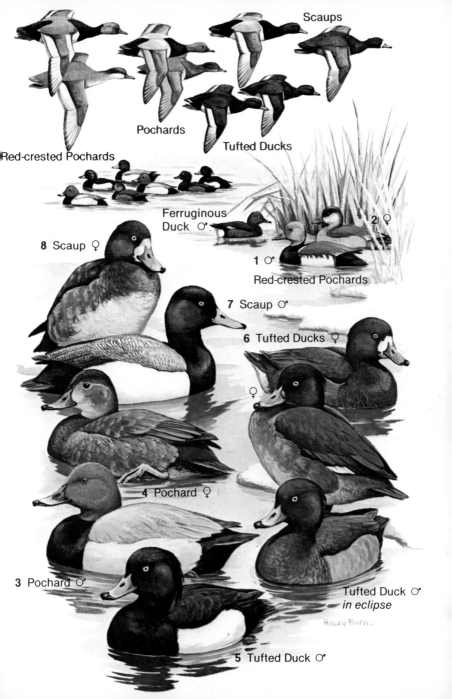

Scaups

Pochards

Tufted Ducks

Red-crested Pochards

Ferruginous Duck ♂

1 ♂

2 ♀

Red-crested Pochards

8 Scaup ♀

7 Scaup ♂

6 Tufted Ducks ♀

♀

4 Pochard ♀

3 Pochard ♂

Tufted Duck ♂
in eclipse

5 Tufted Duck ♂

Hilary Burn

Eider *Somateria mollissima*

These are 'sea ducks', a term used to describe species of duck which spend most of their lives on the open sea.

Eiders nest in the open, often on rocky islands. Nests are lined with downy feathers plucked from the female's breast; this 'down' is still used for eiderdowns to keep human beings warm. As soon as the young have hatched and dried, they make their way to the sea. This journey is dangerous as the tiny ducklings are easy prey for predators such as gulls, but once on the water they can escape by diving.

For a few days the young are guarded by their mothers, but the ducklings can feed only in shallow water, while adults need deeper water: soon, the young of various families join together in crèches with a few ducks in attendance, while the rest of the adults go off to feed.

The powerful bill of the Eider is used for pulling mussels and other shellfish off rocks; these molluscs are swallowed whole and ground up in the bird's gizzard.

Long-tailed Duck *Clangula hyemalis*

There can be few more exciting and beautiful sights than a flock of Long-tailed Ducks on a stormy sea in winter. The spectacular winter plumage of the male is, however, only one of three distinct plumages, but the others are usually only seen on the Arctic breeding grounds.

This species regularly breeds farther north than any other species of duck. It feeds on shellfish which are found by diving up to 20 m underwater.

The loud cooing call of the male has led to the bird's North American name of Oldsquaw.

Ruddy Duck *Oxyura jamaicensis*

This small diving duck belongs to a group of ducks known as 'stiff-tails'. It is native to North America and those seen wild in Britain are descended from about 70 young which escaped from the Wildfowl Trust's collection at Slimbridge in Gloucestershire between 1956 and 1963. They then colonised parts of the English midlands and have now spread to new areas.

The male Ruddy Duck has a remarkable display; he cocks his tail, raises two tufts of feathers on his head and inflates an air-sac in his neck; he then rapidly drums on his swollen neck with his bill, which creates a hollow sound and also produces many air bubbles on the surface of the water.

Eider
Size of Mallard – 60 cm. Large, wedge-shaped bill. Male (**1**) is white with black underparts and black crown. Green marks on back of head and rosy flush on breast. Female (**2**) is brown. Young males and males in moult (**3**) have a variety of dark brown and white plumages.
Breeds around rocky coasts in northern Britain. Also seen around southern coasts in winter.

Long-tailed Duck
Smaller than Mallard – 44 cm, but tail of male may be extra 13 cm. Small, neat duck with small bill. Male (**4**) is brown in summer with pale flanks and white face patch. Largely white in winter (**5**) with dark patch on cheek. Female (**6**) has dark body, pale head with dark smudge on cheeks. No wing-bar in flight.
Visits inshore waters in winter, mainly in Scotland, northern England and Ireland.

Ruddy Duck
Much smaller than Mallard – 39 cm. Male (**7**) is reddish-brown with darker head, white cheeks, white undertail and blue bill. Female (**8**) is brown, has buff cheeks with dark line under the eye. Both sexes have stiff projecting tails which may be cocked or lowered onto the water. *Breeds on inland lakes mainly in central England but currently colonising new areas.*

Long-tailed Ducks

Ruddy Ducks

Eiders

5 *winter* ♂

4 *summer* ♂

Long-tailed Ducks

immature ♂

6 ♀

1 Eider ♂

3 Eider ♂
moulting

2 Eider ♀

7 ♂

8 ♀

Ruddy Ducks

Hilary Burn.

Common Scoter *Melanitta nigra*

On looking out to sea in winter it is not unusual to see flocks of dark brown and black ducks swimming, diving and flying low over the waves. These are Common Scoters, mostly winter migrants from Iceland and northern Europe.

Common Scoters are true 'sea duck' and feed by diving for shellfish. Underwater, they use their feet for propulsion, but their wings are partly opened, which helps to steady them in their search for food on the sea bed.

As scoters spend so much time on the open sea, especially in the North Sea and in busy shipping lanes, they regularly fall victims to oil-slicks.

Velvet Scoter *Melanitta fusca*

The Velvet Scoters which visit our coastal waters in winter come here from their feeding grounds in Scandinavia or the northwest USSR. Largest numbers are to be found in January and they start leaving their winter quarters in March.

Vast numbers of Velvet Scoters gather, in late July, off the coast of Denmark where they undergo their annual moult. The whereabouts of the wintering areas for many of these birds remains a mystery.

Goldeneye *Bucephala clangula*

The species gets its name from its beautiful golden eyes which are usually difficult to see unless one happens to get very close. Most Goldeneyes are winter visitors from northern Europe, but since 1970 increasing numbers have nested in Scotland. The nest is usually 10–15 m off the ground in a hole in a tree-trunk. They will also readily adopt nest-boxes; the erection of these around suitable lochs in central Scotland has helped the species to colonise.

During late winter and early spring, it is not unusual to see Goldeneyes displaying. Groups of several drakes gather with one or more ducks in attendance. The drakes throw back their heads, displaying their brilliant white breasts while they make a low growling call.

The curious hump on a Goldeneye's head contains chambers of air, which, it is thought, give the bird a reserve air supply to enable it to dive for longer periods.

Common Scoter
Smaller than Mallard – 49 cm. Male (**1**) is only all-black duck, with yellow and black bill with a knob at its base. Female (**2**) is dark brown with paler cheeks, throat and neck. Neither sex shows any wing-bar in flight.
Flocks seen in coastal waters in winter. A few pairs nest in western Scotland and Ireland.

Velvet Scoter
Size of Mallard – 55 cm. Male (**3**) is black with white wing-patch sometimes visible, white mark under eye and orange side to its large bill. Female (**4**) is dark brown with white wing-patch and often patches on head. White wing-patches very noticeable in flight.
Seen on the sea in winter, often with Common Scoters and Eiders.

Goldeneye
Smaller than Mallard – 46 cm. Male (**5**) is black-and-white, with glossy green sheen to its black, domed head, white patch between bill and eye, and black back. Female (**6**) is greyish with brown head and white collar.
1st-winter (**7**) is like female, but browner with no collar. Wings make whistling noise in flight. Both sexes show white wing-patches in flight.
Seen around coasts and on inland lakes in winter. A few pairs breed in Scotland.

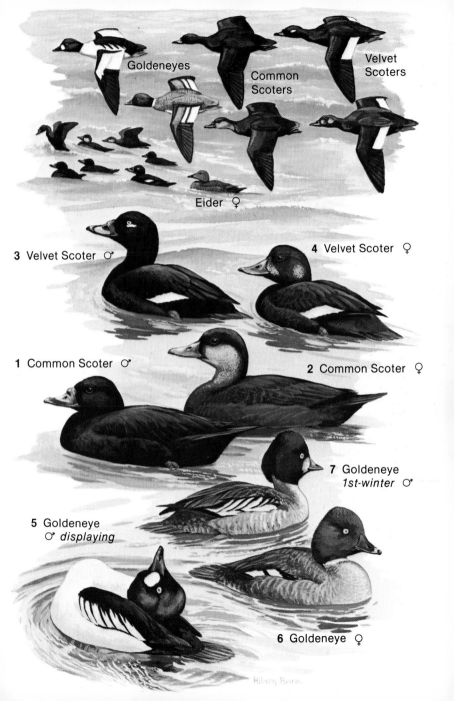

Goldeneyes

Common Scoters

Velvet Scoters

Eider ♀

3 Velvet Scoter ♂

4 Velvet Scoter ♀

1 Common Scoter ♂

2 Common Scoter ♀

7 Goldeneye *1st-winter* ♂

5 Goldeneye ♂ *displaying*

6 Goldeneye ♀

Hilary Burn

Smew *Mergus albellus*

The Smew, or 'White Nun' as the male of this beautiful winter visitor from the USSR used to be called, is a member of a group of ducks known as 'sawbills' (see below). Of the three sawbills likely to be seen in Britain, the Smew is the rarest.

The crest on the drake's crown is raised during courtship. Like other sawbills, Smews eat fish, but they also feed on insect larvae and shellfish, which they find by diving up to a depth of about 4 m.

Red-breasted Merganser *Mergus serrator*

Although Red-breasted Mergansers have nested in Scotland and Iceland for centuries, they started nesting in England only in 1950 and in Wales in 1953, and more recently have spread farther south.

Unlike other ducks, sawbills chase fish underwater, and their long, narrow bills with serrated edges help them to catch and hold their slippery prey. When fishing they often look for prey by submerging their bill and eyes below the surface. Sometimes a group of mergansers will fish together, hunting in circles or semicircles and diving at the same time: a profitable method if a shoal is discovered.

Red-breasted Mergansers nest on the ground, and line their nests with grey breast feathers. Goosanders, which nest in holes, use paler feathers as a nest-lining as they have less need for camouflage. After hatching, large groups of young from different broods sometimes gather together with a few females, known as 'aunties', to look after them.

Goosander *Mergus merganser*

The Goosander, our largest sawbill, is a relative newcomer, being only a rare winter visitor 100 years ago; it was first found nesting in 1871 in Scotland and in England in 1941. Its arrival was not welcomed by fishermen who were concerned about the possible effect on fish stocks, but, in spite of persecution, it became established and continues to expand its range in Britain, recently reaching Wales.

Where there are trees, the Goosander regularly nests in holes up to 18 m from the ground; in treeless areas, the female nests among rocks near water. Young ducklings are often carried on the female's back.

Like other ducks, the drake has an eclipse plumage, and from July to late September he resembles the female.

Smew

Much smaller than Mallard – 26 cm. Male (**1**) is white with black mask and other black lines. Female (**2**) is grey with reddish-brown head and contrasting white cheeks and throat. Black-and-white wing-pattern shown by both sexes in flight.
A few visit inland lakes in winter. Occasionally seen on the sea.

Red-breasted Merganser

Mallard-sized – 55 cm. Long, thin bill and wispy crest. Male (**3**) has green head, chestnut breast and white collar. Female (**4**) has grey body, pale throat blending into brown, and brown head merging with grey neck. In flight, white wing-patches shown by both sexes, but larger patch of male is crossed by black bars.
Breeds in northern and western parts of British Isles, often on lakes or rivers away from the coast. Visits coasts and estuaries in winter.

Goosander

Larger than Mallard – 62 cm. Long body and long, thin red bill. Male (**5**) is pinkish-white, with dark green head and black back. Female (**6**) has drooping crest, well-defined white throat and marked division between brown head and grey neck. Male has black-and-white wings in flight, female square wing-patches.
Breeds on lakes and rivers in northern Britain. Visits southern lakes and reservoirs in winter.

Red-breasted Mergansers

Goosanders

Smews

6 ♀

Goosanders

1st-winter

5 Goosander ♂

4 Red-breasted Merganser ♀

4 ♀

Red-breasted Mergansers

3 ♂

1 Smew ♂

2 Smew ♀

Hilary Burn.

Marsh Harrier *Circus aeruginosus*

Once, there were many large fens and marshes in Britain where Marsh Harriers were common, but, gradually, reedbeds were drained to make more farmland, and these spectacular birds of prey became rare. As they declined, their eggs were taken by collectors and many were shot, stuffed, mounted and displayed in glass cases; eventually, they ceased to nest here. Several years passed before they returned to Norfolk where, under protection, they survived and spread to a few other East Anglian marshes.

The chief prey is small mammals and waterbirds. Males are sometimes polygamous, having more than one mate. Like other harriers, the male will often call the female off the nest; she will then rise, fly behind and below him and catch the prey which he drops.

Although some Marsh Harriers are seen in Britain in winter, most are summer visitors and migrate to Africa. Many never complete the journey because they are shot by hunters in southern Europe.

Hen Harrier *Circus cyaneus*

Happily, a Hen Harrier quartering rolling moorland is no longer an unusual sight. Having been persecuted in the last century, this harrier made a successful comeback from its stronghold in the Orkneys, and, at a time when many birds of prey were declining, it was actually recolonising northern Britain and Ireland.

When hunting, harriers fly slowly, a metre or two from the ground, taking a zig-zag course into the wind. Ears, as well as eyes, are used to locate a small bird or mammal in the dense vegetation. Harriers are among the few day-flying raptors which use their ears to help them find their prey and it is assumed that their keen hearing is further aided by the owl-like disc round their face.

A male Hen Harrier may have a territory of a square kilometre or more and within it have several mates, the record number apparently being seven females. In winter, Hen Harriers often gather together in the evenings and roost communally.

Montagu's Harrier *Circus pygargus*

First identified by Colonel George Montagu in 1802, this, our rarest harrier, has steadily declined since the 1950s and now only a small number are seen each year and few, if any, pairs rear young.

Female and young Hen and Montagu's Harriers look very similar; they are jointly known as 'ring-tails'.

Marsh Harrier

Size of Buzzard – 48–56 cm. Largest harrier. Long wings, long tail and long legs. Often flies low with wings in shallow V. Male (**1**) has dark body, yellow head, grey tail and grey on wings. Female (**2**) is dark brown with straw-coloured head and fore-wings, juveniles (**3**) similar, but may be all-brown. *Mainly a summer visitor, breeding in a few reed-beds in eastern Britain.*

Hen Harrier

Smaller than Buzzard – 44–52 cm. Male (**4**) is silver-grey with white underparts, black wing-tips and a white rump. Female (**5**) is larger, and is brown with white rump. Often hunts low over the ground. Wings held in shallow V when soaring. *Breeds on moorland in northern and western British Isles. Visits open country in other areas in winter, especially near the coast.*

Montagu's Harrier

Smaller than Buzzard – 43–47 cm. Male (**6**) is grey with pale underparts and streaks on belly and flanks; has black wing-tips and a black wing-bar. Rump is pale grey. Female (**7**) is brown with white rump, often smaller than similar patch on Hen Harrier. Pale patch behind eye and dark cheeks. Juvenile (**8**) has rufous underparts, sometimes streaked on sides of breast. *Rare summer visitor to moorland and marshes mainly in southern Britain.*

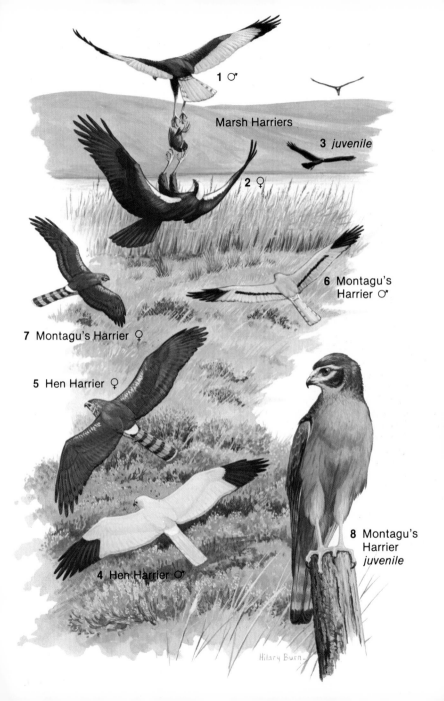

1 ♂

Marsh Harriers

3 *juvenile*

2 ♀

6 Montagu's Harrier ♂

7 Montagu's Harrier ♀

5 Hen Harrier ♀

4 Hen Harrier ♂

8 Montagu's Harrier *juvenile*

Hilary Burn

Goshawk *Accipiter gentilis*

Once extinct as a British breeding bird, the Goshawk now breeds here again and, if left undisturbed, may recolonise even more of our forests in future.

In Britain, Woodpigeons and crows are common prey and mammals up to the size of hares may also be killed. Prey is usually seized after a fast, low, short flight.

Sparrowhawk *Accipiter nisus*

A hunting Sparrowhawk often chooses a flock of small birds. Using the cover of nearby trees, bushes or hedges it will move closer until, suddenly, it makes a short dash to pick on perhaps the slowest bird, which is pursued, seized by a large yellow foot, carried away, plucked and eaten.

This secretive raptor has been persecuted, and also suffered from the effects of harmful pesticides. The population appears to be recovering and Sparrowhawks are now once again to be found in many of our woods.

Birds such as finches and thrushes are the chief prey, but the much larger female may take birds up to the size of a Woodpigeon. A few mammals are also eaten.

Buzzard *Buteo buteo*

Whether soaring effortlessly or sitting patiently on a telegraph pole, Buzzards are impressive as they are the largest raptor that many of us ever see. Once very common, they were persecuted in the last century and declined, but since then they have recolonised some of their former haunts and may spread to other areas provided gamekeepers observe the bird protection laws and resist the temptation to shoot, trap or poison them.

Buzzards hunt from a perch, from the ground or while hovering. Rabbits are an important food. In the 1950s, when the disease myxomatosis killed many rabbits, Buzzards also decreased for a time. Other food includes small mammals, especially voles, carrion, insects and even earthworms.

In early spring, pairs display near crag or tree nest-sites. Birds spiral upwards, the lighter male climbing fastest and then diving at the female.

Rough-legged Buzzard *Buteo lagopus*

A buzzard of the Arctic tundra which migrates south in winter and may visit coastal areas of eastern Britain. Occasionally, larger numbers arrive in autumn; these invasions may be triggered by food shortages in the breeding areas.

Goshawk
Much larger than Sparrowhawk – 48–62 cm. Female (**1**) is Buzzard-sized. Male (**2**) is smaller. Relatively short, broad rounded wings and long tail. White stripe over eye and dark cheeks gives hooded appearance. White undertail-coverts. Flies low to ground or soars; when soaring, hind edge of wing is S-shaped.
Rare breeding species in a few large woods.

Sparrowhawk
Smaller than Woodpigeon – 28–38 cm. Female (**3**) larger than male. Short, rounded wings, long tail and barred underparts. Adult male (**4**) has slate-grey upperparts and orange-tinged underparts. Typical flight is a dash through woods or along hedges. Also soars.
Lives in woodland.

Buzzard (5)
Large raptor – 54 cm. Female slightly larger than male. Broad wings, short neck and short, rounded, barred tail. Variable plumage: upperparts brown, paler underparts with dark wing-patches. Often soars with wings held in shallow V. Has 'mewing' call.
Lives mainly in northern and western Britain and in northern Ireland.

Rough-legged Buzzard (6)
Size of Buzzard – 55 cm, with longer wings and tail. Variable plumage, but usually pale underparts contrasting with dark belly-patch, tail-band, wing-patches and wing-tips.
Sometimes winters in eastern Britain.

1 ♂
Goshawks
2 ♀

♀
♂
Sparrowhawks

Buzzards

Rough-legged
Buzzard

Buzzard

6 Rough-legged
Buzzard

4 Sparrowhawk ♂

3 Sparrowhawk ♀

5 Buzzard

Red Kite *Milvus milvus*

Once, Red Kites were common scavengers, even on the streets of London, but improved sanitation, loss of suitable habitat and, most important, persecution by man, almost wiped out the species. Only ten pairs remained in central Wales at the beginning of this century.

The hanging oak woods in the steep-sided valleys of central Wales are still the Red Kite's stronghold. Special protection has helped the population recover slightly, but egg-collectors still raid nests, birdwatchers and tourists accidentally disturb nesting pairs, and upland feeding haunts are lost through planting with conifers.

Kites eat carrion, especially dead sheep, but also kill small mammals, insects and worms.

Golden Eagle *Aquila chrysaetos*

The Golden Eagle has been cruelly persecuted and the Scottish Highlands are now its only stronghold in Britain. Recently there has been some recolonisation, including a few birds nesting in northern England.

Golden Eagles feed mainly on mammals and birds, especially hares, Ptarmigan and Red Grouse. Carrion is also frequently eaten. When hunting, these eagles range over an area of 4,000–5,000 hectares.

Usually two eggs are laid in the traditional eyrie in March. There is an interval of several days between the eggs hatching, and in most cases the elder chick kills the younger. The reason for this behaviour is not clear, but may be connected with shortage of food.

In spite of legal protection, these birds are still killed by keepers and breeding pairs are often disturbed by climbers, walkers and even birdwatchers.

Osprey *Pandion haliaetus*

Hunted to extinction in Britain by 1916, the Osprey was a rare visitor until 1954 when a pair nested once again. Since then they have been specially protected. The pair at Loch Garten in Inverness-shire has become world-famous and is visited annually by thousands of tourists.

Ospreys feed on fish, which are located from the air and caught after a spectacular aerial dive during which the bird plummets down head first, and at the last moment the feet are thrown forward to seize the fish. The bird is well adapted: its nostrils can be closed, plumage is waterproof, talons are long and curved and there are spines under its toes to help grip the slippery prey.

Red Kite (1)
Larger than Buzzard – 63 cm. Long forked tail, long wings with pale patches on undersides. Pale head, dark back and reddish underparts. Very manoeuvrable in flight. Often glides on flat wings and flexes tail.
Breeding restricted to central Wales; rare elsewhere. Nests in old oak woods.

Golden Eagle
Much larger than Buzzard – 80 cm, wingspan over 2 m. Large and powerful. Long wings are held in shallow V when soaring, or flat when gliding. Tail is long and head protrudes well in front of wings. Adult (2) is dark brown with yellow head and neck. Immature (3) has white base to tail and white patches in wings.
Nests on crags, sea cliffs or in trees. Found mostly in Scottish Highlands.

Osprey (4)
Slightly larger than Buzzard – 56 cm, with longer wings. Dark brown above and white below. Streaked breast and dark patches on underside of wings. Dark mask and slight crest. Often soars; wings have bowed appearance resembling those of a large gull. Plunges feet-first for fish.
Usually seen between April and September. Breeds in pines near Scottish lochs and seen farther south mostly on migration in spring and autumn.

1 Red Kite

Osprey

3 Golden Eagle
immature

2 Golden Eagle
adult

Buzzard

Osprey

4 Osprey

Hilary Burn.

Peregrine *Falco peregrinus*

The popularity and fortunes of the Peregrine have changed over the centuries. In the Middle Ages, when hunting with falcons was very common, the Peregrine was a symbol of royalty or nobility and specially protected by severe penalties. Later, when game shooting became popular, Peregrines, like other birds of prey, were treated as vermin and shot and trapped.

During World War II, homing pigeons were released by airmen who crashed and, to protect these pigeons, Peregrines which nested on many sea cliffs were destroyed. After the war, the Peregrine population started to recover, but by the 1960s it had declined again until the numbers were reduced by over 50%. The cause of this reduction was found to be DDT and other chemicals used to protect farm crops from insect pests. These 'pesticides' were being used on seeds which were eaten by small birds which were, in their turn, eaten by Peregrines. The build up of chemicals in Peregrines resulted either in their death or, at lower concentrations, in unsuccessful breeding: the eggs, which were often infertile, had such thin shells that they frequently broke during incubation.

Following the withdrawal of the most dangerous chemicals the Peregrine population has slowly increased, although the illegal activities of some gamekeepers, egg-collectors and falconers prevent the number of Peregrines fully recovering in many areas.

Although the Peregrine will catch and kill mammals, it specialises in hunting birds, particularly birds in flight. Its prey may vary in size from Blue Tit to Great Black-backed Gull. The best known method of attack is the 'stoop': Peregrines spot their prey from a high perch or while circling, then they fold back their wings and drop at a very high speed to strike their prey with a foot, often tearing it open with a talon which kills the victim outright or knocks it senseless so that the Peregrine may then recover it from the ground. Sometimes prey is seized in mid-air or occasionally picked skilfully off its perch.

Peregrine
Large and powerful falcon 36–48 cm. Male (**1**) is much smaller than female (**2**). Broad pointed wings, rather short tail. Adult has blue-black back and buff underparts barred with black. Black head and 'moustache', white cheeks and chin. Juvenile (**3**) has dark brown upperparts. Flight is pigeon-like with long glides. When hunting, often drops from great heights and may reach speeds of over 160 kph. Most usual call is a chattering 'kek-kek-kek'. *In summer, Peregrines are found on moorland and other open areas usually near crags or sea cliffs. In winter they visit estuaries.*

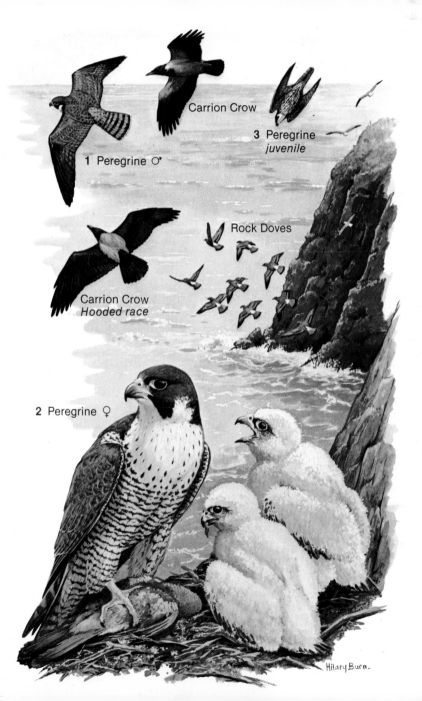

1 Peregrine ♂

Carrion Crow

3 Peregrine
juvenile

Carrion Crow
Hooded race

Rock Doves

2 Peregrine ♀

Hilary Burn.

Kestrel *Falco tinnunculus*

Equally at home hovering over windswept moors, motorway embankments or noisy town centres, Kestrels must be our most familiar bird of prey. In the past, they have suffered many of the problems which reduced the populations of other raptors, yet they have been able to adapt to our rapidly changing countryside.

A Kestrel's diet includes mammals (especially voles), insects, worms and small birds. Hovering, head into the wind, is the most usual method of hunting; when prey is located, the Kestrel glides gently down and, at the last moment, lifts its wings above its back and drops onto the creature. Kestrels often hunt from perches and also catch small birds in flight. They do not limit their hunting to daylight and may hunt at dusk or even after dark, especially on moonlit nights.

Kestrels usually nest in holes in trees, on cliff ledges and on buildings. They will use nest-boxes and, on the Dutch polders, the siting of many boxes has encouraged large numbers of Kestrels to colonise this reclaimed area which lacks natural nest-sites. The Kestrel is the emblem of the Young Ornithologists' Club.

Merlin *Falco columbarius*

This is Europe's smallest falcon. It feeds mainly on small birds, especially Meadow Pipits and Skylarks, which it catches in the air, often after a fast and spectacular chase. At other times, Merlins will surprise their prey and the chase will be short. Sometimes, two Merlins will hunt together and they have also been seen to catch birds which were disturbed by other birds of prey. When food is plentiful, it may be stored and eaten later.

Nest-sites are usually on the ground. Sites may be occupied for many years: one site is said to have been used for 19 years, although the adults were killed by gamekeepers each year and no young were reared.

Hobby *Falco subbuteo*

This small, spectacular falcon is our only bird of prey to feed regularly on large insects, which it catches in flight with its feet. Dragonflies are its favourite prey, but birds such as Swallows, Swifts and Skylarks are also often caught in the air.

Hobbies winter in Africa, south of the Sahara, and return to the heathland, downland or farmland of southern England in April. They nest in trees, often using unoccupied nests of Carrion Crows.

Kestrel
38 cm. Long, pointed wings and long tail. Wings appear more rounded when soaring. Regularly hovers when hunting. Male and female are similar size. Male (**1**) has chestnut back with black spots and blue-grey head and tail, the tail having a black band above its white tip. Female and juveniles are less colourful with darker, barred backs and tails.
Found in most parts of Britain and Ireland, even beside busy roads and in town centres.

Merlin
Smaller than Kestrel – 27 cm. Male (**2**) has bluish back, reddish striped underparts and black band at end of tail. Female (**3**) is larger with dark brown back and bars on tail, but no dark 'moustache'. Flight is dashing, with rapid wingbeats and short glides. Highly agile when chasing prey. Rarely soars and never hovers.
Lives in open country, especially moorland in summer. Often moves to coastal marshes in winter.

Hobby (4)
Size of Kestrel – 33 cm. Shorter tail than Kestrel and longer, scythe-like, wings. Often resembles a large Swift in flight. Dark blue-grey above and heavily streaked below, chestnut flanks and dark 'moustache'. Fast, streamlined and agile in flight, especially chasing large insects or birds.
Summer visitor to open country in southern England.

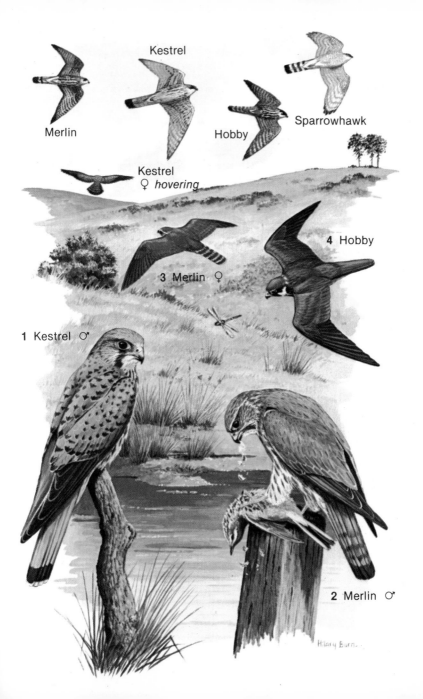

Merlin

Kestrel

Hobby

Sparrowhawk

Kestrel ♀ *hovering*

3 Merlin ♀

4 Hobby

1 Kestrel ♂

2 Merlin ♂

Hilary Burn

Red Grouse *Lagopus lagopus*

Large stretches of moorland are looked after carefully to ensure that grouse survive in sufficient numbers for good shoots in the autumn and winter. It was to protect this valuable gamebird that many birds of prey were slaughtered by gamekeepers in the past and, in some areas, this persecution continues illegally today.

Red Grouse are mainly vegetarian, feeding on heather shoots, flowers and seeds; they will also land in trees and bushes to feed on berries. Young grouse eat insects. Although grouse will move to lower lying farmland in winter, many remain on the moors and burrow in the snow to find food.

All moors may look similar to us, but some are better for grouse than others as these birds require a delicate balance of young shoots for food and old, deep heather for nesting.

Like other young gamebirds, grouse chicks are able to fly before they are fully grown. In summer, while adults are moulting, moors may appear empty as the grouse hide and only occasionally show their heads over the top of the heather.

Very few Red Grouse ever move more than 1.5 km from their breeding areas and it has been proved that the breeding population on any moor is limited to a certain number of cocks which can hold territory; the remaining birds do not move far away, but occupy less favourable habitat where they become weak and easy prey for Golden Eagles, foxes and other predators.

The Red Grouse is the emblem of the journal *British Birds*.

Ptarmigan *Lagopus mutus*

These gamebirds live beyond the moors on the high, barren mountain tops where the wind is keenest, snow lies longest and the vegetation is similar to that of the Arctic. Only the severest winter blizzards drive them down to slightly lower, more sheltered places. They feed on shoots, leaves, berries and seeds of low growing vegetation.

Ptarmigan may easily be seen near the tops of some Scottish ski-lifts. They show little fear of man and will often approach very close. If startled, they are more likely to crouch and 'freeze' than to fly off: their beautifully mottled plumage blends perfectly with the lichen covered rocks. Their main enemies are Golden Eagles, which regularly search the barren tops.

To have three distinct seasonal plumages is unusual among birds, but each provides the Ptarmigan with perfect camouflage which helps it to survive.

Red Grouse
Larger than Grey Partridge – 40 cm. Plump, dark red-brown bird with white stripes on underwings and rounded dark tail. Male (**1**) is redder than female (**2**) and has red wattle over eye. When disturbed, grouse 'explode' from the ground with whirring wings and then glide with bowed wings. Seen in flocks in autumn and winter. Alarm call is a cackling 'kowk-kok-kok'. When displaying, the call sounds like 'Go back-back-back'.
Found on open treeless heather moors and bogs in northern and western Britain and Ireland.

Ptarmigan
Larger than Grey Partridge – 35 cm. Has white wings and underparts and black tail at all seasons; rest of plumage is pure white in winter except that male (**3**) has black mark around eyes. In summer male (**4**) is darker brown than female (**5**) and also has larger red wattle over eye, but in autumn male is grey and female dark brown. Call is a harsh croak and alarm call is a grating sound.
Lives on high, barren mountain tops in central and northern Scotland.

Red Grouse

Ptarmigan

3 ♂ *winter*

4 ♂ *summer*

2 Red Grouse ♀

5 Ptarmigan ♀

1 Red Grouse ♂

Hilary Burn.

Black Grouse *Tetrao tetrix*

Early in the morning, as the sky becomes lighter in the east, the soft crooning calls of the Black Grouse may be heard at the wooded edge of a moor. This is a 'lek', a communal display area where the males, sometimes called 'blackcock', fan their tails, strut around and fight mock battles while the females, or 'greyhens', wait silently nearby. Soon some of them will mate and then the group will melt away.

Black Grouse feed on buds, shoots, leaves, berries and also some insects. They usually feed on the ground, but will also feed in trees, especially when snow covers other plants.

Once Black Grouse were more widespread, but they declined in the last century. In some places they have been reintroduced and, recently, marked increases have been noticed. They do not breed in Ireland, in spite of attempts to introduce them there.

Capercaillie *Tetrao urogallus*

This giant of the pine forests was once common and widespread in Scotland and Ireland, but as forests were felled it became rarer until the last Capercaillie was shot in Scotland in 1785, and the species became extinct in Ireland at about the same time. In 1837–8, Capercaillies were brought from Sweden and reintroduced successfully into Perthshire. Soon there were more reintroductions into other parts of Scotland, although attempts to re-establish the species in Ireland failed.

In spite of their large size, Capercaillies can be surprisingly difficult to observe as they are secretive, and the females are particularly well camouflaged. They feed on shoots and buds of conifers and will frequently perch in trees in order to reach their food. They also roost in trees at night.

Capercaillies display in the early morning for a few weeks in the spring. Several males fly into a traditional site in a forest and there they sing and fight. Many females may be attracted to the display area and it has been found that the larger males are usually dominant and therefore mate with more females.

Black Grouse
Larger than Grey Partridge – male 53 cm, female 41 cm. Male (**1**) is glossy black with white wing-bar and shoulder patch. The male's tail is black and lyre-shaped: under it are white feathers which are shown off during courtship displays. Female (**2**) is larger and greyer than Red Grouse, and has forked tail and slight double wing-bar. Males make dove-like cooing and bubbling calls during courtship. *Favourite habitats are moorland, young conifer plantations, open pine forests or open birch woods. Sometimes visits nearby farmland to feed. Found in Scotland, Wales, parts of the West Country and northern England.*

Capercaillie
Largest gamebird – male 86 cm, female 62 cm. Male (**3**) is huge blackish bird with pale patch on shoulder. Wings are broad and tail quite long and wide. The brown-barred female (**4**) is larger than Black Grouse with reddish patch on breast, pale flanks and rounded tail. Call of male during display is a remarkable series of double notes which end in a loud 'pop'. *Lives in mature Scottish pine forests and in some conifer plantations.*

Capercaillie ♀

Black Grouse
♂
♀

Black Grouse
1 ♂
2 ♀

2 ♀

Capercaillies
3 ♂

4 ♀

Hilary Burn.

Red-legged Partridge *Alectoris rufa*

This partridge is not native to Britain, but has been introduced into many parts of the country between 1673 and the present day. Many of these introductions failed, but some have been successful and it has colonised the drier parts of Britain, especially in the south and east.

Adults feed on seeds, leaves, roots and small numbers of insects; young birds eat many more insects. Red-legged Partridges often form flocks, or 'coveys', and when danger threatens they sometimes run away rather than fly.

The nest is a shallow scrape, lined with vegetation. Males may build several nests – the female will lay her eggs in one of them and then may lay a second clutch in another nest which will be incubated by the male.

Grey Partridge *Perdix perdix*

These partridges are most numerous in traditional mixed farming areas of Britain where fields are small and hedges thick and well cared for. Such farmland is, unfortunately, disappearing: fields are becoming larger, hedges are being uprooted and the Grey Partridge has declined so that, in some places, the introduced Red-legged Partridge is more numerous. Pesticides, which kill the insect food of young partridges, cold weather in spring, and the sowing of cereal crops in autumn, which reduces the number of sawflies, are all thought to have contributed to the decline of the Grey Partridge.

When feeding or at rest, Grey Partridges appear dumpy and may easily be mistaken for large stones or lumps of soil. When alarmed, they will squat, relying on their camouflage to blend in with their surroundings, and only at the last moment take to the air.

Although these partridges feed out in the open, they breed more successfully if their nest is under the cover of a thick hedge or among other dense vegetation. They regularly dust-bathe in dry soil which helps with feather care. Although they are mainly vegetarian, the young eat many more insects than do their parents.

Quail *Coturnix coturnix*

The distinctive call of the male, until he attracts a mate, is usually the only evidence that Quail are present; at all times they are highly secretive.

Quail were once widespread, and their decline is not fully understood. Being migrants, wintering south of the Sahara, they face many dangers on their migratory journeys, not least southern European hunters. In some summers they are far more abundant than in others.

Red-legged Partridge (1)
Larger than Grey Partridge
– 33 cm. Colourful at close quarters. Wax-red legs and bill and striped flanks. Black-and-white face pattern may be seen from a distance. Tail is reddish. Runs swiftly. Often seen in small flocks. Usual call is a repetitive 'chuck-chucker'.
Found on farmland. Most common in southern and eastern England. Also likes dry, sandy places, downland and even open areas in woods.

Grey Partridge
30 cm. Plump, rounded body and domed head. Body is brown-and-grey with an orange-brown face. Male (2) has dark horseshoe mark on lower breast; female (3) has similar but less distinct mark. Tail is reddish. Call is a grating 'krrr-ick' or 'skee-er'. Like other gamebirds, flight is fast with rapid wingbeats followed by a glide on downcurved wings.
Found mainly on farmland in many parts of Britain and Ireland.

Quail
Much smaller than Grey Partridge – 17 cm. Very secretive, usually located by 'whip, whip-whip' call (said to sound like 'wet my lips') heard particularly at dawn and dusk. Sandy-brown plumage with buff streaks, no barring on flanks, cream stripe on top of head and over eye. Male (4) has dark streaks on throat.
Rather rare summer visitor to corn- and hayfields mainly on the chalk downlands of southern England.

1 Red-legged Partridge ♂

Grey Partridges

Red-legged Partridges

Quails

4 ♂

2 ♂

Grey Partridges

3 ♀

Hilary Burn.

Pheasant *Phasianus colchicus*

The original home of the Pheasant was between the Black Sea and China, but it was first introduced into England by the Normans in the 11th century and later was introduced into Scotland, Wales and Ireland. Pheasant numbers are unnaturally high in areas where they are hunted as they are still bred in captivity and released; Pheasants are far fewer in places where there are no gamekeepers or shooting interests.

In the past, the protection of Pheasants meant the destruction of birds of prey, but now the law protects these predators. There are other benefits from shooting, as woods and covers which are preserved for Pheasants are also often oases for wildlife that would have difficulty in surviving in otherwise bleak farmland.

Pheasants' food includes grain, seeds, berries, roots, shoots and insect larvae. Most food is found on the ground where Pheasants spend most of the day, but at night they generally roost in trees, away from ground predators such as foxes.

Golden Pheasant *Chrysolophus pictus*

The natural home of this colourful pheasant is the mountains of central China. The first ones were brought to Britain in the 18th century, but Golden Pheasants were not encouraged to breed wild until the end of the last century and, even now, despite many attempted introductions, they are firmly established in only two areas: the Brecklands of East Anglia, and Galloway.

In spite of the male's colourful plumage, Golden Pheasants are difficult to observe. They are long-legged and agile, slipping easily through dense vegetation.

Lady Amherst's Pheasant *Chrysolophus amherstiae*

Named after the wife of a Governor General of India, who sent specimens of this pheasant to London from which the species was first identified. Lady Amherst's Pheasants are native to the high mountain slopes of southwest China and Tibet. The species was introduced into Britain in about 1900 and has successfully colonised a few young conifer plantations, and mixed and deciduous woodlands, especially where there is dense undergrowth.

Lady Amherst's Pheasants are extremely secretive, and observation in the wild in Britain is very difficult: if disturbed, they will often run or skulk rather than fly.

Pheasant
Male – 75 cm. Female – 60 cm. Plump, with small head, long neck and long tail. Typical male (**1**) is large and colourful with white collar and long pointed tail. Interbreeds with other races, resulting in a variety of plumages. Female (**2**) is sandy-brown with darker marks and long tail (but shorter than male's). Flies with rapid wingbeats followed by a glide. Runs with tail cocked. Male's crowing call is 'korrk-kok' followed by loud rustling wings. *Resident in farmland, parkland and woods in most parts of British Isles.*

Golden Pheasant
Male – 100 cm. Female – 70 cm. Smaller bodied than Pheasant, but with longer tail. Male (**3**) is very brightly coloured. Female (**4**) is like female Pheasant, with domed head and longer, downcurved tail. Rarely flies. Crowing call is more high pitched than Pheasant's. *Secretive, living in coniferous woods, mainly in East Anglia, and a few other places.*

Lady Amherst's Pheasant
Male – 110 cm. Female – 80 cm. Exotic-looking male (**5**) has very long black-and-white tail. Female (**6**) is like female Golden Pheasant, but less golden and has horn-coloured bill and blue-grey feet. Call is similar to Golden Pheasant's. *Found in dense woods mainly in Bedfordshire.*

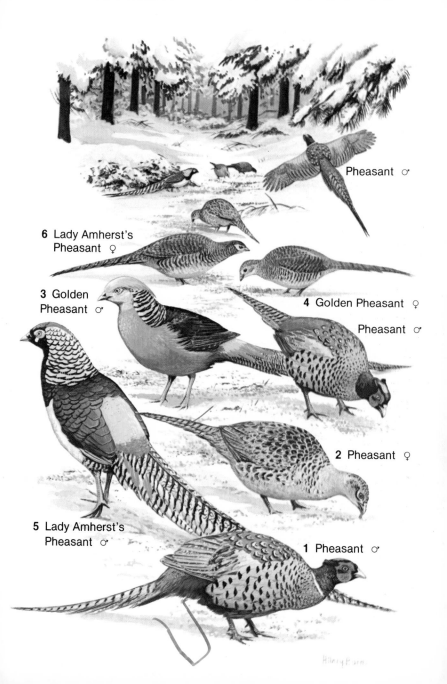

Pheasant ♂

6 Lady Amherst's Pheasant ♀

3 Golden Pheasant ♂

4 Golden Pheasant ♀

Pheasant ♂

2 Pheasant ♀

5 Lady Amherst's Pheasant ♂

1 Pheasant ♂

Water Rail *Rallus aquaticus*

A reedbed can be a frustrating place for the birdwatcher: birds move to and fro and are often only glimpsed by the observer; various noises are heard, yet the creatures which make them remain hidden. The Water Rail is one of the birds likely to be skulking in a reedbed and its strange calls may be heard by day or by night.

Our Water Rails do not migrate, but those living farther north and east migrate in the autumn and return again in spring. Britain and Ireland, therefore, receive an additional winter population.

Water Rails are extremely slim birds and move through dense vegetation with ease, leaving no obvious paths. In winter, they may be forced out of their normal habitat by floods or by ice.

Although Water Rails swim frequently, they usually feed in shallow water. Their food is mainly animal matter such as insects or small fish, although shoots, roots and fruits are also eaten.

The Spotted Crake *Porzana porzana* is an extremely secretive wetland species which may breed in just a few parts of Britain. It is small, the dark body is flecked with white spots and the bill is yellow with a reddish base. Its persistent 'h'wit, h'wit' call sounds rather like a whiplash and is most likely to be heard after dark.

Corncrake *Crex crex*

Once, the grating call of the Corncrake would have been a familiar summer sound in farmland throughout the British Isles, but the species has steadily declined since the middle of the last century. Changes in farming techniques and drainage of wet areas are blamed for its decline, not only in the British Isles, but also in much of northern and western Europe.

Corncrakes in flight appear weak, but this is far from the truth, as they are long-distance migrants. Migrating at night, they are capable of long journeys with little or no rest and they spend the winter in Africa, probably south of the Equator. Flying from southern Africa to northern Europe is very risky, but Corncrakes face an extra hazard; because they fly low they frequently collide with overhead wires and cables which cover so much of western Europe.

Water Rail
Smaller than Moorhen – 25 cm. Secretive, with long, red bill, long legs and large feet. Upperparts of adult (**1**) are brown with black streaks. Face, neck and underparts blue-grey. Whitish feathers under tail. Flanks are barred black-and-white. Flight is weak, with legs trailing. Juvenile (**2**) has pale stripe over eye, pale throat and dark bill which may appear short. Variety of calls including grunts and a pig-like squeal.
Water Rails live in reedbeds and other dense waterside vegetation in many parts of the British Isles.

Corncrake (3)
Smaller than Moorhen – 28 cm. Yellowish-buff with darker marks on back and chestnut wings. Appears short-necked; bill is short. Greyish on head and breast. Very secretive. Its loud repetitive 'crek-crek' song can be simulated by drawing a comb across the edge of a wooden ruler. This strange noise (from which the bird gains its scientific name *Crex crex*) is heard mainly after dark, but also during the day. *Summer visitor to hayfields and other areas with tall vegetation mainly in western Scotland and Ireland.*

Corncrake

3 Corncrakes

Moorhen
juvenile

1 *adult*

Water Rails

2 *juvenile*

Hilary Burn

Moorhen *Gallinula chloropus*

Wherever there is fresh water there will probably be Moorhens (sometimes called Waterhens) nearby. Reed-beds, farm ponds, muddy ditches and edges of large reservoirs are home for this familiar species. Only north-west Scotland and a few other upland areas have not been colonised because Moorhens usually avoid fast-flowing water or pools with little or no cover.

Moorhens are often skulking and shy and may be difficult to observe, yet in parks, and other places where they become accustomed to people, they may be very tame. Much of their time is spent among waterside vegetation and on land searching for food, which includes pondweed and other water plants, berries, snails, insects, small fish and even the eggs of other birds.

In early spring, Moorhens often build display platforms, where much of the courtship takes place, and later one of these is converted into a nest in which the eggs are laid. Once the young have hatched, they move to one or more specially constructed 'brood nests' as an alternative to their true nest. Two or three broods may be reared in a summer and juveniles of early broods may help to feed the young of the later ones.

Coot *Fulica atra*

A first glance might show little difference between Coot and Moorhen: both may be found on the same lake and one might wonder if these two related species compete for the same food. In fact, they could hardly be more different.

While the solitary Moorhen searches for food among waterside vegetation, flocks of Coots gather on open water and find most food by diving one or two metres below the surface. Moorhens' toes are long and thin for climbing; Coots' toes are partly webbed for swimming and diving efficiently.

Coots feed on plants, seeds and insects and also take eggs of other birds. Although most food is found in water, flocks of Coots sometimes feed on land, especially in winter. They are highly territorial and very aggressive. Fights are easy to spot as the quarrelling birds appear to sit on their tails and strike at each other with wings, feet and bills.

When breeding, Coots usually choose lakes with waterside vegetation from which they build a nest. In winter, flocks visit reservoirs, even those with concrete banks, where they may be joined by migrant Coots from northern and eastern Europe, including the USSR.

Moorhen

33 cm. Adults (**1**) look black with red-and-yellow bill, white line along flanks and white under the tail. The tail is constantly flicked when swimming or walking. Head jerks backwards and forwards when swimming. The long legs and large feet are yellow-green. Juveniles (**2**) are browner than adults, with white throat and chin and less distinct line along flanks. Has a variety of throaty calls including the familiar 'crorrk'.
Lives near fresh water, from small ponds to large lakes, in most parts of the British Isles.

Coot

Larger than Moorhen – 37 cm. Adult (**3**) is all-black waterbird with white bill and forehead. Rounded head and rounded back. Tail sits flat on water, not flicked like Moorhen's. Large grey-green feet are lobed. Juvenile (**4**) is dark grey with whitish throat, neck and belly. Most common call is a hollow-sounding 'kwok' (said to resemble 'coot', hence its name). Patters along water surface to get airborne and flies with legs trailing.
Found mainly on large areas of fresh water in most parts of the British Isles except northwest Scotland.

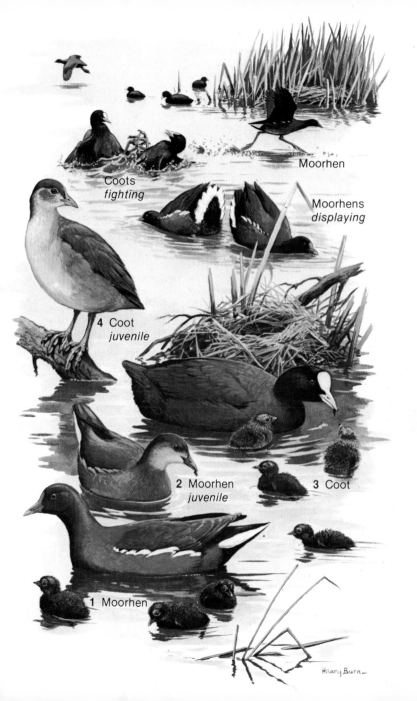

Coots
fighting

Moorhen

Moorhens
displaying

4 Coot
juvenile

2 Moorhen
juvenile

3 Coot

1 Moorhen

Hilary Burn

Oystercatcher *Haematopus ostralegus*

These birds may not feed on oysters, but they do eat shellfish, especially mussels, cockles and limpets. The powerful bill is used to stab or prise open shells; individuals specialise in these two different feeding techniques, which are imitated by their young. This species differs from most other waders in that it feeds its young instead of letting them feed themselves.

Breeding all around our coast, Oystercatchers are absent only where feeding is difficult or where there are too many holidaymakers. Nesting inland is a recent development; at first they spread up some large Scottish rivers, but soon moved to nearby farmland. This change was possible because Oystercatchers feed on earthworms. More recently, some inland gravel workings in southern Britain have also been colonised.

Migrant Oystercatchers from Iceland and northern Europe winter on our estuaries. Some are long-lived: one German bird is known to have survived 34 years.

Avocet *Recurvirostra avosetta*

There can be few more attractive sights than a pair of Avocets with young. For many years, this could only be seen abroad, as the species became extinct in Britain in the middle of the last century. Fortunately, Avocets returned and, as a result of protection by the RSPB, it is now possible to watch them on reserves such as Havergate Island and Minsmere, both in Suffolk. So successful was the protection that the RSPB has adopted the Avocet as its symbol.

Avocets do not probe the mud with their beaks as do most other waders; instead, they sweep their bills from side to side and filter tiny shrimps or insect larvae from the water, or delicately snap up a small creature. Feeding usually takes place in shallow water, but Avocets can wade through deep water and will sometimes swim or even up-end, like ducks, to reach food.

Stone-curlew *Burhinus oedicnemus*

In the 1950s, myxomatosis wiped out most of Britain's rabbit population and long grass and bushes began to grow on the bare areas where Stone-curlews had nested. That, together with more intensive farming and the planting of conifers on other nest-sites, resulted in the species' decline.

Stone-curlews are active by night and one of the best times for hearing their eerie call is 3 o'clock on a spring morning.

Oystercatcher
Larger than Lapwing – 43 cm. Adult in summer (**1**) is a distinctive black-and-white wader with long orange-red bill and pink legs. Broad white wing-bar shows in flight. Juvenile and adult in winter (**2**) have white collar. Call is loud 'kleep-kleep'.
Seen around the coasts of Britain and Ireland in summer and winter. Also, nests inland in Scotland and northern England.

Avocet
Size of Oystercatcher – 43 cm. Adults (**3**) are black-and-white, with slim, black, upswept bill and long, blue-grey legs. The feet are webbed. Fully grown juvenile (**4**) resembles adult, but is browner. Call is a fluty 'kleep'.
Rare breeding species needing shallow pools near the coast in order to breed. Winters on sheltered estuaries in southern Britain.

Stone-curlew (5)
Larger than Lapwing – 41 cm. Sandy brown with darker streaks, rounded head with large yellow eyes, long thick legs and short bill. Ungainly bird, often standing hunched up. In flight, two bold whitish wing-bars are very noticeable. Call is Curlew-like 'coo-ree', often to be heard at night.
Rare summer visitor to sandy heaths and chalk downland mainly in southeastern England. Seen elsewhere on migration.

Avocet

Oystercatchers

4 *juvenile*

5 Stone-curlews

Avocets

3 *adult*

2 *winter*

1 *summer*

Oystercatchers

Little Ringed Plover *Charadrius dubius*

There are few better examples of a species taking advantage of a newly created habitat than the Little Ringed Plover and its colonisation of gravel workings.

This attractive, small plover generally nests farther south than the Ringed Plover and its traditional habitat is inland shingle banks near rivers. New gravel diggings offer a similar habitat.

Soon after they return to the breeding grounds in March or April, their display flight may be seen: the long, slow wingbeats as the bird zig-zags to and fro. As with other small plovers, this species benefits from 'disruptive' camouflage, the bold pattern helping to break up the outline against a background of shingle.

Ringed Plovers sometimes breed in the same locality as Little Ringed Plovers and, where this occurs, the larger species may dominate.

Ringed Plover *Charadrius hiaticula*

This familiar species is also found in the High Arctic. Ringed Plovers which nest in the British Isles are the most southerly population, except for a few in France. Our Ringed Plovers are mainly resident, but those breeding farther north are long-distance migrants, and some of these pass through our islands en route to winter quarters in southern Africa.

In recent years, more Ringed Plovers have started to nest on farmland near the coast instead of on the beaches where they nested in the past. This move from the coast may be the result of disturbance by holiday-makers.

When feeding, Ringed Plovers, like several other species, have developed a special technique known as foot-pattering: the bird rapidly vibrating wet mud with its foot. This habit appears to encourage prey, such as worms, to come to the surface, perhaps in the mistaken belief that it is raining!

Kentish Plover *Charadrius alexandrinus*

Since 1956, this attractive species has ceased to breed regularly in Britain, although some still visit the south and east coasts, and occasionally a pair may nest. The Kentish Plover is widespread in Europe, and one reason for its decline in Britain may be disturbance of its breeding grounds by holiday-makers.

Although Kentish Plovers were first discovered breeding in Kent, the name is misleading as they do not nest there now, and they winter in Africa.

Little Ringed Plover
Smaller and more delicate than Ringed Plover – 15 cm. Adult (**1**) has white line above black forehead and yellow eye-ring. No wing-bar shows in flight. Legs are yellowish-green. Call is fluty 'pee-oo'. Juvenile (**2**) has scaly back and incomplete breast band.
Summer visitor, mainly to sand and gravel workings in many parts of England.

Ringed Plover
Smaller than Redshank – 19 cm. Adult (**3**) has black-and-white head pattern and black breast band. Legs are orange. White wing-bar shows in flight. Juvenile (**4**) has scaly back, lacks the head pattern of adult and has an incomplete breast band. Feeding birds run swiftly, stop suddenly and whole body tilts forward when food is sighted. Call is an attractive 'too-li'.
Found mainly on shingle and sandy seashores, but nests inland in some places.

Kentish Plover
Smaller than Ringed Plover – 16 cm. Adult has black bill and usually black legs, narrow black eye-patch, dark patches on sides of breast and white wing-bar in flight. Male (**5**) has rusty crown. Female (**6**) is paler. Juvenile (**7**) resembles female and usually has dark legs. Beware confusion with young Ringed Plovers with muddy legs!
Rare visitor, mostly in spring and autumn, to shingle or sandy beaches.

Kentish Plover

Ringed Plovers

Ringed Plovers

Little Ringed Plover

6 Kentish Plover ♀

7 Kentish Plover *juvenile*

5 Kentish Plover ♂

2 Little Ringed Plover *juvenile*

1 Little Ringed Plover

3 Ringed Plover

4 Ringed Plover *juvenile*

Hilary Burn

Lapwing *Vanellus vanellus*

The small flocks of Lapwings which are to be seen in the countryside in June or July are migrants from Europe and often the first indication that, for some species, the breeding season is over and autumn migration has begun.

Numbers of Lapwings continue to build up during late summer and autumn as more arrive from the Continent and join those which nested here. A sudden cold spell, however, will cause many of them to fly south or west, where often the weather is milder and feeding easier. If the cold weather is prolonged, Lapwings will move even farther, to Ireland, France or even Spain. In Spain, the Lapwing is called *'Ave fria'*, the bird from the cold.

Lapwings breed in a variety of habitats, from ploughed fields to the edges of large lakes. In southern Britain, the Lapwing population has declined, probably because of changes in farming practice and the drainage of wet meadows. In the north, the species is still numerous, and may even be increasing.

The Lapwing is such a familiar bird that it has several widely used names, including 'Peewit', which describes its call, and 'Green Plover', which describes the colour of its plumage and its relationship.

In February, many Lapwings begin to display over their territories and it is then that their wheezy, 'peewit' call is most often heard. The male flies slowly over his territory but soon speeds up, until suddenly he climbs steeply, pauses, and then tumbles downwards, straightening out only a metre or so above the ground, and sweeps low over the field before rising and tumbling yet again. During these spectacular manoeuvres, the displaying bird's wings make a far-carrying humming, from which the species' official name, Lapwing, is derived. On the ground, courtship continues, with the orange undertail-coverts playing an important part in the highly ritualised display.

The eggs are laid in a hollow on the ground and are beautifully camouflaged. The chicks also merge with their surroundings. Like other wader chicks, they leave their nest soon after hatching, and, if danger threatens, the conspicuous adult will attempt to distract the predator while the chicks lie still, flat on the ground.

Lapwings feed on insects, grubs, worms, snails, slugs and some seeds. They are, therefore, no threat to any crops and are an attractive addition to many farmers' fields. In winter, they often form flocks together with Golden Plovers on ploughed land, or stubble or old pasture.

Lapwing
30 cm. Black, white and dark metallic green with orange under the tail. At a distance, appears black-and-white. Crest is obvious on adults (**1**) on the ground. Juveniles (**2**) have a scaly back and shorter crest. Usual flight is lazy, wings are broad and rounded with an obvious black-and-white underwing pattern. In display, twists, turns and dives. Call is a wheezy, drawn-out 'peewit'. *Breeds on farmland and other open ground in most parts of the British Isles. Migrants arrive from Europe for the winter.*

Lapwing *display*

Golden
Plover

Golden
Plover

2 Lapwing
juvenile

1 Lapwing
adult

Hilary Burn

Dotterel *Charadrius morinellus*

The summer home of Dotterels is the rounded tops of the highest mountains, where there is little vegetation and snow lies longest. To avoid snow Dotterels nest on wind-swept plateaux, usually 850 m or more above sea level. Strangely, it is the female Dotterel that has the brightest plumage and, once the eggs are laid, it is usually the male which incubates and tends the young while the females gather together in groups.

Unfortunately, some of the best breeding areas are now regularly visited by tourists and nesting Dotterels are often disturbed. Perhaps the best place to see them is at a traditional stopping area, where small groups, known as 'trips', may be seen in lowland fields while on their spring migration; they often visit the same fields each year. In the Netherlands, they have recently started to nest in similar areas, below sea level.

Golden Plover *Pluvialis apricaria*

There are few more beautiful sights or sounds than Golden Plovers displaying over moorland in spring, when they chase each other excitedly or 'switch-back' over their territories and reach a great height while giving their simple but lonely-sounding song. A typical territory contains one or more hummocks or stones which are used by them as lookouts. When danger threatens, adults try to lead the intruder away from nest or young by first running towards the danger, then running away, sometimes dragging a wing and pretending that they are injured.

Both eggs and young are protected by cryptic camouflage so they blend in with the surrounding heather and moss which helps to conceal them from predators.

In favoured areas, where possible nesting territories are fewer than the number of pairs, some Golden Plovers wait their turn to nest until another pair has finished breeding.

Grey Plover *Pluvialis squatarola*

These birds nest on Arctic tundra, but small numbers may be seen on British and Irish estuaries at most seasons of the year, especially in September when migration is at its height. When feeding they are usually well spaced out, but high tide forces them off their feeding grounds and then they may gather at regular high-tide roosts.

Their diet includes shellfish, insects, and crustacea such as crabs. Their bills are short, so most food is picked up from the surface of wet mud.

Dotterel
Smaller than Lapwing – 22 cm. Colourful at close range, with chestnut belly. White stripes over eyes which meet at back of head, and a pale breast band. Female (**1**) is brighter than male (**2**). Autumn plumage is browner and marks fainter. Juvenile (**3**) is buff with faint marks and streaked back.
Summer visitor to the tops of our highest hills. Seen in lowland Britain only on migration.

Golden Plover
Smaller than Lapwing – 28 cm. Round-headed with yellow spangled back. In summer has black belly, black breast and face pattern which is more clear-cut on those breeding in northern Europe (**4**) than on those nesting in the British Isles (**5**). Underwing is white. In winter (**6**) belly is pale. Call is a lonely 'pee-ye-we-oo'.
Nests on upland moors. Winters on lowland farmland, often with Lapwings.

Grey Plover
Smaller than Lapwing – 28 cm. Plumper than Golden Plover. Often hunched up and looks 'neck-less'. Breeding plumage (**7**) is black-and-white spotted back, separated from black face and underparts by white line. In winter (**8**), face and underparts are pale, back of adult is brownish-grey. Juvenile is spotted white. Black 'arm-pit' (axillaries) shows in flight. Call is a sad 'tee-oo-ee'.
Visits estuaries and seashores, mainly in autumn and winter; rare inland.

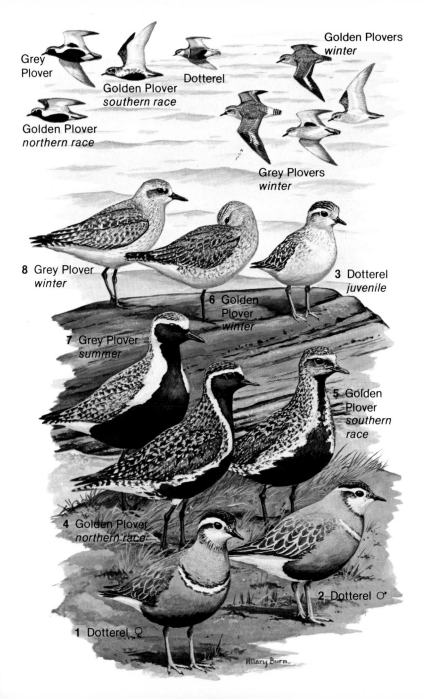

Grey Plover

Golden Plover
southern race

Dotterel

Golden Plovers
winter

Golden Plover
northern race

Grey Plovers
winter

8 Grey Plover
winter

6 Golden
Plover
winter

3 Dotterel
juvenile

7 Grey Plover
summer

5 Golden
Plover
*southern
race*

4 Golden Plover
northern race

2 Dotterel ♂

1 Dotterel ♀

Hilary Burn.

Knot *Calidris canutus*

Over 400,000 Knots, two-thirds of the western European winter population, feed on British or Irish estuaries in autumn and winter. Thousands may be seen twisting and turning together over their feeding grounds or high-tide roosts and looking, from a distance, like clouds of smoke. Closer to, however, their white bellies contrast with their grey backs and flocks flash grey-and-white in winter sunlight.

Most of the Knots which visit the British Isles breed in Greenland, although some come to us from Siberia. Our estuaries are rich in food, and Knots probe in wet sand and mud for small crabs, insects and shellfish.

Sanderling *Calidris alba*

On a sandy beach Sanderlings can often appear like clockwork toys as they run amazingly fast along the edge of the sea, snatching sand-hoppers and other small food items from the tide's edge and, at the same time, dodging the wash from the waves. Sanderlings also probe with their bills in wet sand, often around pools left by an out-going tide. They are frequently seen in small groups and are quite tame; sometimes they mix with other species such as Dunlin and Knot.

The breeding grounds are north of the Arctic Circle and many birds travel through Europe to winter in Africa as far south as South Africa.

Little Stint *Calidris minuta*

The plumage of this delicate wader is very variable and can often be confusing. Little Stints are passage migrants which breed in Europe north of the Arctic Circle and winter as far south as South Africa. Those which visit the British Isles are usually seen between August and October and most are juveniles.

All birds moult most of their feathers at least once a year; the main moult usually takes place after breeding. Because the northern summer is so short, Little Stints, like some other Arctic breeders, suspend their moult until they have reached winter quarters. In the tropics both adults and juveniles can slowly grow new feathers in readiness for their return journey.

Temminck's Stint *Calidris temminckii*

This species winters in Africa and those birds which visit the British Isles on migration are often seen near inland pools. They breed in northern Europe and recently a few have nested in Scotland.

Knot

Larger than Ringed Plover – 25 cm. Plump with straight bill and rather short legs. Usually in flocks, often in very large numbers. Has faint wing-bar. Grey-and-white in autumn and winter (**1**). Brick-red underparts in summer (**2**). Call is low 'knut'.
Mainly on estuaries in autumn and winter.

Sanderling

Larger than Ringed Plover – 20 cm. Plump and active. Rather short, straight bill. In autumn and winter (**3**), has pale grey back, white underparts and sometimes shows black mark on front of wing. Broad white wing-bar. In breeding plumage (**4**), has reddish-brown back, head and breast.
Seen on sandy beaches in autumn and winter.

Little Stint

Smaller than Ringed Plover – 13 cm. Very small with short, fine, black bill. In winter (**5**) has scaly brown back and white breast. 1st-year birds (**6**) have V pattern on their backs. Breeding plumage (**7**) reddish-brown.
Mainly seen in autumn around shallow water.

Temminck's Stint

Smaller than Ringed Plover – 14 cm. Like Little Stint, but less lively when feeding and in autumn (**8**) is greyer, with less scaly back, paler legs and darker breast. Outer tail is white. General appearance when breeding (**9**) rather like small Common Sandpiper.
Rare spring and autumn migrant. A few nest in Scotland.

Dunlin

Knot

Sanderling

Temminck's Stint

Little Stint

Knots

2 Knot *summer*

1 Knot *winter*

Dunlin

3 Sanderling *winter*

4 Sanderling *summer*

9 Temminck's Stint *summer*

5 Little Stint *winter*

8 Temminck's Stint *autumn*

6 Little Stint *1st-winter*

7 Little Stint *summer*

Hilary Burn.

Purple Sandpiper *Calidris maritima*

The name 'Purple' is rather misleading as this colour may be seen only at very close quarters, as a purplish sheen on some of the back feathers.

Purple Sandpipers breed mainly in the Arctic and winter farther north than other waders. Many move hardly any distance after breeding, and winter on northern ice-free coasts, while others move south or west, but only very few travel as far as southern Europe. They search for food on rocky coasts, where they appear to prefer flat rocks projecting into the sea. Often, they mix with Turnstones. Food is mainly small fish, insects, shrimps, shellfish and vegetable matter and is picked up as it is washed ashore. Small groups often feed on the very edge of the sea and somehow manage to dodge the larger waves while ignoring human observers.

Dunlin *Calidris alpina*

It is usually not difficult to see Dunlins around British or Irish coasts in winter: either as a small group feeding together, looking round-shouldered with heads down, probing the mud methodically; or as a wheeling flock, twisting and turning over an estuary.

Dunlin plumage is very variable and so is their length of bill. Those with the shortest bills breed in Iceland. Because the unfeathered parts of a bird lose heat most quickly, bills and legs of populations which live in cold climates tend to be shorter than those of Dunlins living in warmer regions.

Like many other waders, Dunlins forsake estuaries and beaches when nesting and move to moorland. In Britain, they prefer poorly drained moors with scattered pools, although in Ireland they usually nest on lower, wet areas near lakes and marshes.

Common Sandpiper *Actitis hypoleucos*

The shrill 'willy-wicket' call, a glimpse of the typical bow-winged flight, with wings flicking below the level of the body, and then a distant view of the bird bobbing on a partly submerged stone, are usually the first clues that a Common Sandpiper is around.

Fast-flowing upland streams or lochs with stony edges are the normal summer home. Generally, Common Sandpipers are seen only in ones or twos.

Although most Common Sandpipers winter in Africa, some do remain in southern Britain. In spring and autumn migrants are regularly to be seen in most areas, both inland and near the coast.

Purple Sandpiper
Larger than Ringed Plover – 21 cm. A dumpy, often tame, wader with rather short legs, yellow base to bill and a white wing-bar. In winter (**1**), the back is almost black, the head and breast dark brown and the underparts pale with dark marks. In breeding plumage (**2**), the back becomes more scaly and the face paler.
Visits rocky coasts in winter and feeds close to the edge of the sea.

Dunlin
Smaller than Ringed Plover – 18 cm. Common, small wader with variable plumage. Medium length, black bill usually curved down towards tip. Rather short black legs. White wing-bar and white sides to rump and tail. Short-necked and round-shouldered. Reddish-brown back and pale underparts with black belly in breeding plumage (**3**). Greyer in winter (**4**), with white belly. Call, hoarse 'dzee'.
Breeds on damp upland moors. Winters on the coast, especially on mudflats, but also visits inland lakes.

Common Sandpiper (5)
Larger than Ringed Plover – 20 cm. Often bobs, rather like a wagtail. Brownish back, white belly, streaked breast or brown 'smudges' on either side of breast. White wing-bar and white sides to tail in flight. Flies with stiff, bowed wings and also briefly glides. Call is shrill 'tee-we-we'.
Summer visitor to upland lakes and rivers. Visits other areas on migration.

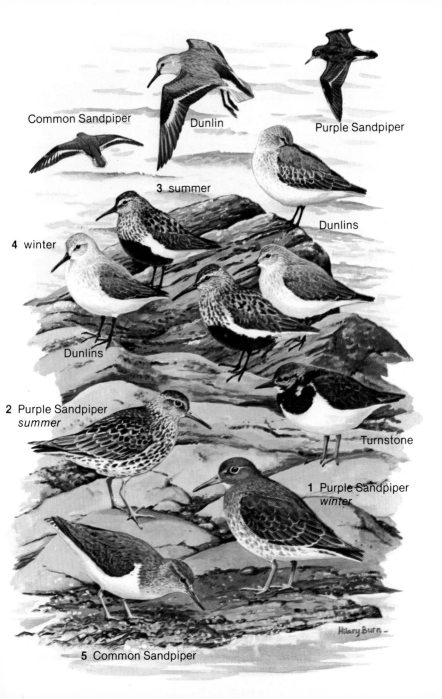

Common Sandpiper

Dunlin

Purple Sandpiper

3 summer

Dunlins

4 winter

Dunlins

Dunlins

Turnstone

2 Purple Sandpiper
summer

1 Purple Sandpiper
winter

Hilary Burn

5 Common Sandpiper

Pectoral Sandpiper *Calidris melanotos*

The Pectoral Sandpipers which visit the British Isles are North American birds which breed in Alaska and northern Canada and normally winter in South America. Some, however, cross the Atlantic by accident during migration, particularly in autumn.

Ruff *Philomachus pugnax*

Before so many of our wet meadows were drained for farming, Ruffs were much more numerous than they are today. As the wetlands disappeared, the numbers of breeding Ruffs also declined until the species became extinct as a British breeder earlier this century. In 1963, however, Ruffs were found nesting on the Ouse Washes on the Cambridgeshire–Norfolk border and a few pairs have nested regularly, both on the Ouse Washes and a few other sites, ever since.

Male Ruffs return to their breeding grounds from Africa in March and the females, known as 'reeves', return a few weeks later. They assemble at display areas, called 'leks', in the early morning: the males, sporting their exotic breeding plumage, display silently, sometimes fighting mock battles and often 'freezing' for short periods. It appears that the males with darker neck feathers are more successful at attracting reeves than are those with white feathers.

Once mating has taken place, the reeves are left to incubate the eggs and look after the young, while the males moult out of their bright breeding plumage.

Outside the breeding season, Ruffs may be seen around the margins of inland and coastal lakes where they feed on insect larvae, small shellfish and seeds. Some Ruffs spend the winter in southern Britain.

Pectoral Sandpiper (1)
Size of Ringed Plover – 19 cm. Longer neck than many other small waders. Similar to Ruff, but smaller, with finer, slightly downcurved bill. Brown back with pale 'Snipe-like' stripes. Streaked breast which ends abruptly above white belly. Legs are greenish-yellow. In flight, tail has dark centre. 'Zig-zag' flight like Snipe when disturbed.
Rare visitor, mostly in autumn in Ireland and western Britain. Visits shallow pools, both near the coast and inland.

Ruff
Larger than Ringed Plover–male 29 cm, female 23 cm. A confusing wader with a variety of plumages and a size difference between male and female. Shorter bill than Redshank. Appears 'round-shouldered' when feeding, but very upright when alert. Female (2) and male in winter (3) have grey-brown backs with buff-edged feathers and buff underparts. Leg colour very variable, from green to orange, but usually brownish. In flight there is slight wing-bar and also black centre to tail with white oval patches on each side. Male in breeding plumage (4) has warty face and colourful 'ruff'.
Rare breeding species of low-lying, wet, grassy meadows. At other seasons visits wet, marshy places.

4 Ruffs ♂

♀

Ruffs

3 Ruff ♂

2 Ruff ♀

1 Pectoral Sandpiper

Hilary Burn

Jack Snipe *Lymnocryptes minimus*

While walking through a wet field in winter you are likely to disturb feeding Snipes, which will fly off as you approach. Sometimes, after the Snipes have flown, the smaller Jack Snipes will also take to the air, almost from under your feet, and then land again not far away. So good is their camouflage, however, that, even if you see where they land, they can be almost impossible to observe among the dense vegetation.

Even when Jack Snipes feed undisturbed, they seldom move far from cover. They bob and sway which helps them to blend with their surroundings.

Snipe *Gallinago gallinago*

'Drumming' is the name given to the strange, bleating sound which Snipes make with their outer tail feathers as they 'switchback' over their territories in spring. The outer tail feathers are formed in such a way as to produce vibrations when air rushes past them; this noise carries over a surprisingly large distance.

A female Snipe incubates her own eggs without help from the male. After the eggs hatch, the young quickly leave the nest and the brood is split, with each parent taking care of a few chicks. This division of the brood means that at least some of the chicks may escape being caught by predators such as stoats. Although young Snipes take seven weeks to grow fully, they are able to fly after two weeks and this gives them extra protection. A Snipe feeds mainly on worms which it locates underground by using its long bill to probe into the moist soil. It cannot see its prey, but the tip of the bill is sensitive and flexible which enables the bird to locate and grasp its food.

Woodcock *Scolopax rusticola*

The best time to see Woodcocks is at dusk or dawn in spring and early summer when males perform their display flight known as 'roding', flying 10–15 m above the ground and following a regular route over one or more woods. Flight is slow and deliberate and may look rather owl-like.

Woodcocks' camouflage is superb and they are very difficult to observe in their woodland home. When feeding, Woodcocks walk slowly, bobbing and swaying. When disturbed they sometimes carry their young from danger between their legs.

In winter Woodcocks in northern Britain move west to Ireland or south to southern England. Others from northern Europe cross the North Sea to winter in Britain.

Jack Snipe (1)
Size of Ringed Plover – 19 cm. Smaller than Snipe, with shorter bill and shorter legs. Walks with a bobbing action. Crown is dark with pale stripes on either side. Often reluctant to fly, but when disturbed usually takes off silently, without zig-zagging, and usually lands again close by.
Visits marshy fields, ditches and edges of lakes in winter.

Snipe (2)
Larger than Ringed Plover – 27 cm. Very long bill and rather short legs. Brownish plumage with paler stripes on back and pale stripe through centre of crown. Underparts are buff. When disturbed, it flies with a zig-zag flight and makes a distinctive 'scraap' call. In spring, it makes a bleating sound during its display flight, and also a 'chipa-chipa-chipa' call, given from the ground or in flight.
Breeds in wet places such as rushy fields and wet upland moors. Visits other wet places in winter.

Woodcock (3)
Larger and plumper than Snipe – 34 cm. Has long bill, short legs and beautifully camouflaged plumage with dark bars across the crown. Rounded wings are obvious in the display flight at dusk when the most common calls may also be heard: a loud, short 'tsiwick' and a soft croak.
Lives in woods with dense ground cover. Will feed in more open places at night.

Woodcock

Snipe *drumming*

Snipe

Jack Snipe

Snipes

2 Snipe

1 Jack Snipe

3 Woodcock

Hilary Burn.

Black-tailed Godwit *Limosa limosa*

This large wader, with long bill and long legs, has become more common as a winter visitor to our coasts and especially to estuaries in the south of the British Isles during this century.

The Black-tailed Godwit is increasing as a breeding species here: once widespread, it became extinct as a British breeding bird, but in the early 1950s it returned and nested at the Ouse Washes on the Cambridgeshire–Norfolk border. Since then, other pairs have bred there and at a few other sites.

When feeding, godwits either wade in deep water or probe in soft mud for insects, worms or shellfish.

Bar-tailed Godwit *Limosa lapponica*

Like many of the waders which do not breed in the British Isles, Bar-tailed Godwits may be seen throughout the year. Most are passage migrants which visit our estuaries to feed in spring and again in late summer. A few non-breeders may remain around our coasts during the summer, and some winter here while the rest migrate to southern Europe or Africa.

Although Bar-tailed and Black-tailed Godwits may feed side by side on British or Irish estuaries and eat similar food, they nest in quite different areas: the Bar-tailed breeds much farther north, in Scandinavia and Siberia, while the Black-tailed breeds in central Europe.

Curlew *Numenius arquata*

Its lonely-sounding call, which gives the Curlew its name, is usually heard as the bird rises steeply and hangs on trembling wings before sailing downwards again. Fortunately, Curlews are more widespread than they were a hundred years ago, when most nested only on moorland; now many breed in lowland areas.

Outside the breeding season, they live on the coast where they feed mainly on shellfish, small crabs, shrimps and lug-worms. The long bill is used either to pick up food from the surface or for probing in wet mud or sand. Like other waders, Curlews eat most of their prey whole, and indigestible parts are regurgitated in the form of pellets.

Whimbrel *Numenius phaeopus*

This small northern 'curlew' has recently increased in numbers in Shetland and also nests on some other northern islands. Elsewhere it is seen mainly as a passage migrant stopping en route to and from its winter quarters in Africa.

Black-tailed Godwit
Smaller than Oystercatcher – 41 cm. Large wader with long legs which project beyond tail in flight. White tail ends with black band. White wing-bar is obvious in flight. Back and breast reddish in breeding plumage (**1**); grey in winter (**2**).
Rare breeding bird of damp meadows or moors. Visits coasts and estuaries at other times.

Bar-tailed Godwit
Smaller than Black-tailed Godwit – 38 cm. No wing-bar and bill often noticeably upswept. Feet project only slightly beyond tail in flight. Tail is barred and rump is pale. In winter (**3**) is similar colour to Curlew. In breeding plumage (**4**) breast and underparts are chestnut-red.
Mainly seen on coasts between August and March.

Curlew (5)
Largest wader – 55 cm. Streaky brown with very long, downcurved bill and no obvious head markings. Very pale rump shows in flight. Call: 'croo-wee' and a loud bubbling song.
Breeds on moors and wet meadows; at other times found around coasts.

Whimbrel (6)
Similar to Curlew, but smaller – 41 cm with shorter bill. Has two dark bands divided by pale streak on crown. Call is a series of seven high-pitched whistles.
Breeds on moors in the north of Scotland. Visits coasts on migration.

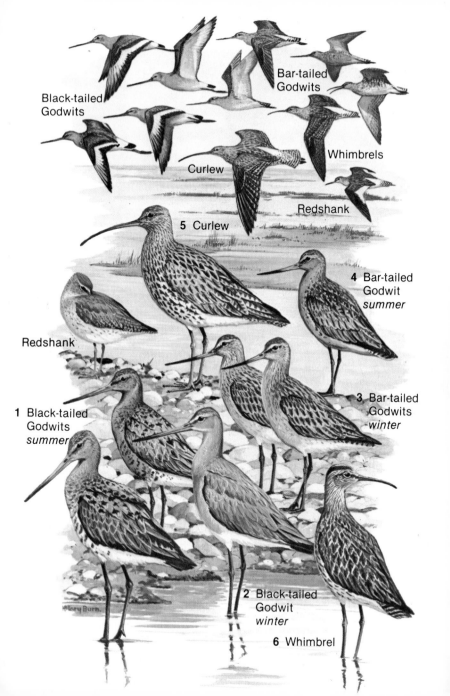

Black-tailed Godwits

Bar-tailed Godwits

Curlew

Whimbrels

Redshank

5 Curlew

4 Bar-tailed Godwit *summer*

Redshank

3 Bar-tailed Godwits *winter*

1 Black-tailed Godwits *summer*

2 Black-tailed Godwit *winter*

6 Whimbrel

Spotted Redshank *Tringa erythropus*

The great difference between breeding and non-breeding plumages of Spotted Redshank may be seen in late summer when birds return from their Arctic breeding grounds and moult on some of our estuaries.

Behaviour is rather like that of the Redshank. It is usually seen in ones or twos and occasionally in small flocks near the coast.

On its northern breeding grounds, it is the male which mostly incubates the eggs and looks after the young.

Redshank *Tringa totanus*

This active, noisy wader is found around shallow water where it feeds on insects, shellfish, worms and some vegetation. The Redshank's nest may be some way from water and the newly hatched chicks are taken on the often dangerous journey to water. One brood was seen to travel 2 km in 24 hours, successfully negotiating walls, roads, fences and a ditch, the adult carrying the young over a wall between its legs.

The Redshank's old name, 'watchdog of the marshes', is well deserved as it is usually the first wader to fly when humans approach and its alarm is a warning to other birds. Although often seen singly or in small numbers, Redshank sometimes nest in small colonies and may be seen in flocks near the coast in winter. Like other waders, Redshank often swim when feeding or when crossing deep dykes or channels.

In spring, salt marshes often ring with the calls of displaying Redshank, flying with fast, shallow wing-beats. When landing they often settle with wings raised for a few moments, displaying vivid white underwings.

Greenshank *Tringa nebularia*

The Greenshank breeds in wild country: from rough, boggy, moorland slopes with occasional clumps of trees, to forest edges and even, sometimes, within woodlands.

In much of Britain and Ireland the Greenshank is only seen as a passage migrant: stopping to feed and to moult partly before completing its journey to the Mediterranean or even to southern Africa where it spends the winter.

The long, slightly upcurved, bill is not only used for probing in wet areas or for picking up food from the surface, but is also often swept from side to side as the bird catches insects and other small creatures.

Spotted Redshank
Larger than Redshank – 30 cm, but more slender with longer red legs and longer bill. Breeding plumage (**1**) is black with white spots. In winter (**2**) has mottled grey back and paler underparts. Pale V-shaped rump extends up back. Unlike Redshank, it has no white on wings. Call is loud 'chew-it'.
A passage migrant which visits wet places, often near coasts, mainly between July and October, but also seen in spring. A few winter here.

Redshank
Smaller than Oystercatcher – 28 cm. Medium-sized wader (**3**) with long red legs, slender bill with red base, brown back with darker marks and pale underparts. In flight shows large white stripe along hind edge of wings, and white rump. Call is a loud, ringing 'tew' or 'teuk' or 'teup' often repeated and slurred. *Breeds on damp marshes or grassy fields. Common around the coast.*

Greenshank
Larger than Redshank – 30 cm. Slim, long necked wader with long greenish legs and long, thick, slightly upturned bill. Back is very dark in spring (**4**), but is greyer at other times (**5**). In flight there is no wing-bar, but long V-shaped pale rump extends up its back. Call is loud 'tew, tew tew'. *Nests inland in the north of Scotland. Visits edges of lakes and coastal marshes elsewhere in spring and autumn.*

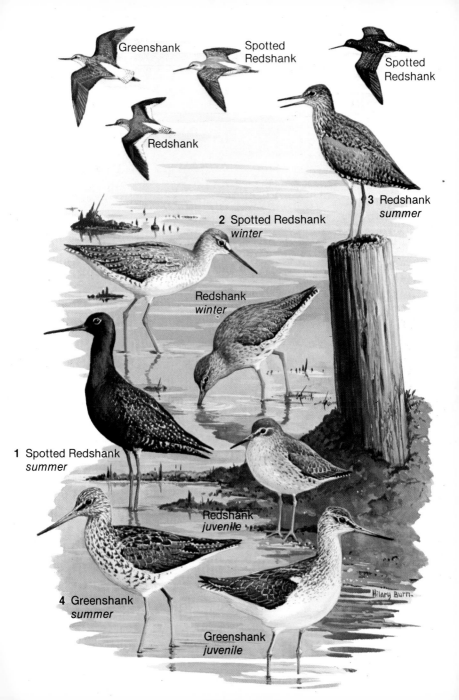

Greenshank

Spotted Redshank

Spotted Redshank

Redshank

3 Redshank *summer*

2 Spotted Redshank *winter*

Redshank *winter*

1 Spotted Redshank *summer*

Redshank *juvenile*

4 Greenshank *summer*

Greenshank *juvenile*

Hilary Burn

Curlew Sandpiper *Calidris ferruginea*

These birds are long-distance migrants. They breed in the northern and northeastern USSR and many migrate to southeast Asia or Australia, while others travel southwest and winter around the Mediterranean or in Africa.

On migration these birds fly at about 65 kph and travel hundreds of kilometres non-stop. In order to make these amazing journeys they must put on extra reserves of fat which gives them the energy required. One study has shown that Curlew Sandpipers wintering in South Africa increase their weight from 53 grams to 80 grams in about eight weeks, which should enable them to fly more than 3,000 km before stopping and feeding again.

Wood Sandpiper *Tringa glareola*

The Wood Sandpiper is most often seen as a passage migrant between July and September, with some arriving in the British Isles in spring. They are usually seen singly or in small groups. Wood Sandpipers breed in northern Europe and winter in Africa.

A few pairs nest in northern Scotland where they breed in wet moorland. Elsewhere they also occupy damp woodland clearings and even use the old nests of tree-nesting birds.

Green Sandpiper *Tringa ochropus*

A shy wader which may sometimes be flushed accidentally from the edge of a lake or river, when all that is usually seen are the long, blackish wings and upperparts and a glowing white rump as the bird flies erratically away, looking like a large House Martin.

On the ground, Green Sandpipers often feed in shallow water with vegetation nearby or where they are sheltered by banks. Like Common Sandpipers, they often bob.

The Green Sandpiper has been found nesting in northern Britain, and may do so again. Instead of nesting on the ground like most other waders, it regularly uses the old nests of other birds, especially thrushes.

Curlew Sandpiper
Size of large Dunlin – 19 cm. Longer legs and longer neck than Dunlin. Downcurved bill and white rump. Breeding plumage (**1**) is brick-red with mottled back. In autumn (**2**) is similar to Dunlin. Juvenile (**3**) has brownish-grey back with rounded pale edges to feathers giving 'scallop pattern', buff breast and white underparts. Wing-bar shows in flight. Flight call is soft 'chirrup'.
Passage migrant to coasts and inland marshes especially in late summer.

Wood Sandpiper (4)
Smaller then Redshank – 20 cm. Medium length bill. In flight no wing-bar, but white rump is obvious; underwing paler and legs longer and extend farther beyond tail than Green Sandpiper's. Back is brownish with white spots. Flight call is 'chiff-if-if'.
Passage migrant, seen near coasts and inland marshes mainly in late summer. More often seen in eastern Britain.

Green Sandpiper
Smaller than Redshank – 23 cm. Medium length bill, dark greenish-brown upperparts and no wing-bar. In flight bold white rump contrasts with dark back; underwing darker than Wood Sandpiper's. Adult (**5**) has spotted back in summer (**6**). Flight when disturbed is Snipe-like and the call is a shrill 'weet-a-weet'.
Mainly a passage migrant, visiting freshwater margins in late summer. Some winter in the south.

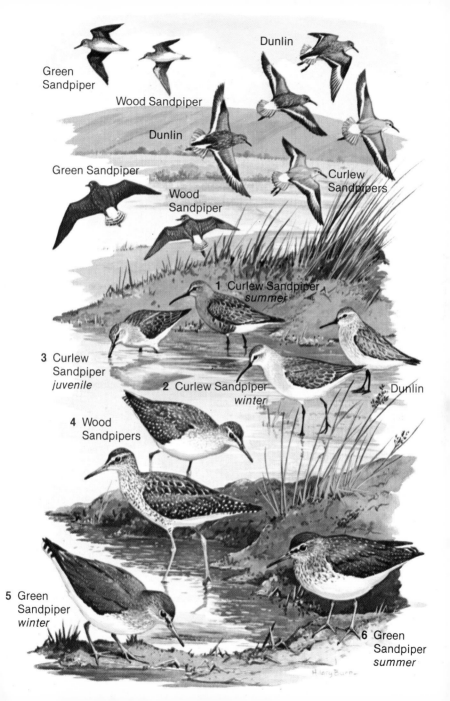

Green
Sandpiper

Wood Sandpiper

Dunlin

Dunlin

Green Sandpiper

Wood
Sandpiper

Curlew
Sandpipers

1 Curlew Sandpiper
summer

3 Curlew
Sandpiper
juvenile

2 Curlew Sandpiper
winter

Dunlin

4 Wood
Sandpipers

5 Green
Sandpiper
winter

6 Green
Sandpiper
summer

Turnstone *Arenaria interpres*

Its habit of using its stout bill to probe under stones, often pushing them aside in its search for food, has given the Turnstone its name. Turnstones feed on insects and other invertebrates, many of which live under stones. By hunting in this way, these birds find food which other waders do not reach.

Turnstones are usually seen in small groups, but larger flocks sometimes form at high tide. They often perch on man-made objects projecting from the water.

Turnstones have never been proved to breed in Britain. Those which are seen here breed either in northern Europe or in Greenland. Most of the northern European ones winter on the west coast of Africa and are passage migrants in Britain; those which spend the winter here are mainly from Greenland.

Red-necked Phalarope *Phalaropus lobatus*

As with the Dotterel, the roles of the male and female phalarope are largely reversed: the female is more brightly coloured and performs the courtship display; the male incubates the eggs and looks after the young.

The scientific family name, *Phalaropus*, means 'coot-footed' and the specific name, *lobatus*, also refers to the bird's partly webbed feet which help it when swimming. Phalaropes often spin round rapidly on the water, which helps to stir up food, which they then pick from the surface.

Only a few pairs nest in Britain each year, mostly in Shetland and on a few other islands off northern Scotland. They are remarkably tame and often allow observers to approach very close. The migration of Red-necked Phalaropes is still partly shrouded in mystery, but most winter at sea, off the coast of Africa.

Grey Phalarope *Phalaropus fulicarius*

Known in North America as the Red Phalarope, this attractive wader is rarely seen in Britain in its colourful breeding plumage. It breeds mainly north of the Arctic Circle in North America and Siberia, with a few nesting in Iceland. Like the Red-necked Phalarope, it spends the winter at sea. It also frequently swims in the phalarope's typical, buoyant manner, often 'spinning' and quickly snatching prey from the surface of the water.

Usually, Grey Phalaropes are seen in ones and twos, but sometimes hundreds appear, having been blown into inshore waters during migration.

Turnstone
Larger than Ringed Plover – 23 cm. Short, stout bill and short, orange legs. Has broad breast band. In summer (**1**) back is black-and-chestnut and the head white with dark marks. In winter (**2**) head and back are blackish. In flight has white marks on wings, back and tail. Call is twittering 'kitititit'. *Usually seen on rocky sea-shores or mussel-beds, and throughout the year.*

Red-necked Phalarope
Smaller than Dunlin – 17 cm. Long, fine, black bill. Usually seen swimming. In summer female (**3**) is brighter than male (**4**); both have grey head, white chin, chestnut neck and a dark back with bold stripes. In winter (**5**) back is grey with paler marks. The head is white with a dark crown and dark cheeks. Juvenile (**6**) has brownish back with buff stripes and buff breast. *A few pairs breed in damp grassy places in northern Scotland.*

Grey Phalarope
Larger than Dunlin – 20 cm. Larger than Red-necked with shorter, stouter bill. In summer (**7**) has chestnut underparts, white cheeks and stripy back. In winter (**8**) is like Red-necked but with plain grey back and less black on crown. 1st-winter (**9**) is like winter adult, but has stronger pattern on back. *Unusual passage migrant found both inland and on coast, especially after westerly gales.*

Grey Phalarope

Red-necked
Phalarope

Turnstone

2 Turnstone
winter

1 Turnstone
summer

7 Grey Phalarope
summer

9 Grey Phalarope
1st-winter

8 Grey Phalarope
winter

4 Red-necked
Phalarope ♂

5 Red-necked
Phalarope
winter

6 Red-necked
Phalarope
juvenile

3 Red-necked
Phalarope ♀

Hilary Burn

Pomarine Skua *Stercorarius pomarinus*

An aerial pirate which is regularly seen off our coasts in autumn. 'Poms' breed in the Arctic, and winter in the open ocean.

Long periods of 'sea watching' are usually necessary to see these birds. The best time is when strong winds off the sea force them into inshore waters, but even then identification (especially of juveniles) is difficult and only with practice can one pick out differences from the other skuas, such as the broader, more rounded wings and powerful flight of a typical 'Pom'.

Arctic Skua *Stercorarius parasiticus*

Skuas are the pirates of our coasts, often chasing other seabirds in the air in order to make them drop their food. The chief victims are terns and the smaller gulls. This behaviour is known as kleptoparasitism. When not harrying seabirds, Arctic Skuas feed on carrion, berries, insects and eggs or young of other birds; they also chase and kill small birds and mammals.

Arctic Skuas breed in colonies on northern moorland, usually close to the sea. Animals such as sheep or dogs and even human beings are likely to receive a vicious attack if they enter the territory of an Arctic Skua.

Colour phases of these skuas vary from pale to very dark. In Britain, most of the breeding birds have dark plumage, the paler phases becoming more common in northern and eastern Europe.

Long-tailed Skua *Stercorarius longicaudus*

The Long-tailed Skua is the smallest and most graceful skua. It breeds in the Arctic and is a rather rare visitor to British and Irish coasts, where it is seen mainly off western Scotland and Ireland and the east coast of England.

Like other skuas, the Long-tailed will harry other birds in flight, but on its northern European breeding grounds it feeds mainly on lemmings.

Great Skua *Stercorarius skua*

The old Viking name of 'Bonxie' is still widely used for this species, both in Shetland and by birdwatchers elsewhere. Bonxies declined in their Shetland stronghold in the last century, but were protected and have recovered so that now there are colonies on other islands and on the Scottish mainland. Migrants may be seen from coastal headlands, especially in good sea-watching weather (mist, drizzle or rain) when they may be closer to the shore and fly low over the sea.

Pomarine Skua
Smaller than Herring Gull – 51 cm. Larger and more bulky than Arctic Skua with a heavier bill. Adult has 'spoon-like' central tail feathers and usually a dusky breast band. Both light (**1**) and dark (**2**) phases may be seen. Chases other seabirds. *Mainly spring visitor to Channel and western coasts; autumn migrant to North Sea coasts.*

Arctic Skua
Smaller than Herring Gull – 46 cm. Colour phases vary from pale (**3**) to very dark (**4**). Adults have long central tail feathers. Flight is graceful and rather hawk-like. Wings have white flashes near tips. Juvenile (**5**) is rich brown with pale barring. *Summer visitor to northern and western Scotland. Seen in other coastal areas on migration.*

Long-tailed Skua
Smaller and more graceful than Arctic Skua, but adult (**6**) has longer central tail feathers – 55 cm. Juveniles (**7**) have grey-brown back, neatly barred with cream or white, and longish, blunt-tipped central tail feathers. *Passage migrant to coasts, mainly in autumn.*

Great Skua (8)
Size of Herring Gull – 58 cm. Rather like large, heavy, short-tailed gull. Often looks uniform dark brown with white wing-flashes. Flight looks slow and heavy, but is fast and powerful when attacking. *Breeds in northern Scotland. Seen around coasts on migration.*

6 Long-tailed Skua

Arctic Skua

1 Pomarine Skuas
light phase

7 Long-tailed
Skua
juvenile

Great Skua

2 Pomarine Skua
dark phase

3 *light phase*

5 *juvenile*

Arctic Skuas

Pomarine
Skua
juvenile

4 *dark phase*

8 Great Skua

Hilary Burn

Black-headed Gull *Larus ridibundus*

The name 'sea-gull' should never be used to describe a Black-headed Gull as this species, more than any other gull, is more at home in a town park than flying over the open sea. The history of Black-headed Gulls in London provides fascinating evidence of how a successful species can adapt to a new environment.

Before 1880, Black-headed Gulls were seen only around the Thames estuary, but from that year they started to move up river, and by the end of the century they were seen regularly along the Thames and its tributaries. The species became more widespread in the early 1900s and by 1917 Black-headed Gulls were catching bread thrown to them from a hotel window! Large winter roosts grew up on some of the reservoirs and in 1940 a breeding colony was discovered on a large London sewage-farm. The invasion of London has been repeated in towns and cities throughout the British Isles.

'Black-headed' is hardly a fair description of a bird which has a mainly white head for almost half the year, and during the other half a dark brown one. The brown head is the breeding plumage and is used in display: when lowered and thrust forward, it is a sign of aggression; when held upright and turned away it is a sign of surrender.

Colonies vary in size from under ten to over 20,000. Within the colonies, pairs occupy small territories, which are defended by ritualised displays. Colonies give protection to nests and all the gulls in the colony are able to take advantage of local food supplies.

Most of the Black-headed Gulls which breed in Britain and Ireland are resident, although they may move around the country in winter. Our birds are joined by migrants from northern Europe and the USSR which arrive from early August onwards.

Black-headed Gulls feed on a wide range of food, including fish, worms, carrion and seeds. When ants are swarming, these gulls, and other birds, may be seen flying erratically as they catch 'flying ants' in the air. Often they will watch other feeding birds and then move in and rob them of their food. A regular victim is the Great Crested Grebe; Black-headed Gulls hover above a diving grebe and if it surfaces with a fish they swoop down and try to steal it.

Many Black-headed Gulls visit refuse tips, especially in winter when other food is scarce. Because they are so adaptable and exploit so many sources of food, it is not surprising their numbers continue to grow.

Black-headed Gull
The smallest of our common gulls – 36 cm. A slim bird with white stripe along front edge of its pointed wings. Adult has dark brown head in summer (**1**) and a dark smudge behind the eye in winter (**2**). Bill and legs are red. Juvenile (**3**) has ginger-brown on head, back and sides of breast. 1st-winter (**4**) birds have brown bar on wing, dark flight feathers and dark band on tail.
Breeds in colonies around inland lakes and on coastal marshes. Common throughout British Isles at all times of year.

Black-headed Gulls

winter

1st-winter

Lesser Black-backed Gull

Common Gulls

3 juvenile

4 1st-winter

1 summer

2 winter

Hilary Burn.

Black-headed Gulls

Mediterranean Gull *Larus melanocephalus*

The number of Mediterranean Gulls seen in southern Britain has increased since the 1950s. In 1968 a pair was found nesting successfully within a Black-headed Gull colony and since then a few other pairs have nested.

The main breeding colonies are around the Mediterranean and the Black Sea, but it has also nested in western and central Europe.

Little Gull *Larus minutus*

This, the smallest of the world's gulls, is a much more frequent visitor to the British Isles than in the past and in 1975 it attempted to breed here for the first time. The species also started to nest in North America in 1962. Until this recent expansion most nested in Siberia and northern and southeastern Europe.

The migration and movements of Little Gulls still puzzle ornithologists. They may turn up anywhere and at any time of year, although the greatest numbers are seen in spring and autumn. In winter, flocks may suddenly appear near our coasts during severe weather conditions, which suggests that many must winter at sea.

Common Gull *Larus canus*

The Common Gull is another gull which does not deserve the title 'sea-gull'. Many of the 50,000 or so breeding pairs in Britain and Ireland nest far from the sea, and, when breeding is over for the year, these gulls, together with others which migrate here from northern Europe, are just as likely to be seen on a playing-field in the heart of a built-up area as they are standing on a windswept beach.

Although some Common Gulls nest among colonies of Herring Gulls around our coast, many more nest singly or in small groups on moorland, sometimes close to a pool or on shingle near a river. Occasionally they nest off the ground in trees or bushes.

Common Gulls are frequently to be seen feeding on rubbish tips in winter. They will also feed on carrion, even animals which have been killed on roads. Their natural food also includes insects, worms, small mammals and eggs.

Sabine's Gull *Larus sabini*

A graceful small gull which sometimes occurs on our coasts in autumn when en route from its North American breeding grounds to its wintering area of southern Africa. The adult has a dark head in summer and at all ages has a bold, distinctive upperwing pattern and forked tail.

Mediterranean Gull
Size of large Black-headed Gull – 39 cm. More like Common Gull in shape, but looks heavier, with a thicker neck and stouter bill. Adult (**1**) has grey wings with white tips and a black head in summer. In winter (**2**) the head is mainly white with a dark streak behind the eye. 1st-winter (**3**) has more contrasting wing pattern than Common Gull.
Has sometimes nested in southern England and one or two may be seen occasionally elsewhere outside the breeding season.

Little Gull
Smaller than Black-headed Gull – 28 cm. Rather tern-like. Often picks food from the surface of the water in flight. Adult (**4**) has blackish underwing, grey upperwing and black head, but loses most black head-feathers in winter (**5**). 1st-year (**6**) has dark W pattern on back and underwing is pale.
Seen throughout the year, mainly in coastal areas, especially in autumn.

Common Gull
Smaller than Herring Gull – 41 cm, with smaller bill, thinner wings and lighter flight. Upperwings of adult (**7**) are uniform grey with white spots on the black wing-tips. On the ground it is rather elegant, with dark eyes and gentle look. Head is dusky in winter (**8**). 1st-winter birds (**9**) have dusky heads, grey backs, dark outer flight feathers and dark tail-band.
Breeds mainly in Scotland and Ireland. Regular visitor elsewhere.

Kittiwake

9 Common Gull *1st-winter*

Sabine's Gull

5 Little Gull *winter*

8 Common Gull *winter*

Little Gull *juvenile*

2 Mediterranean Gull *winter*

Black-headed Gull *winter*

6 Little Gull *1st-winter*

3 Mediterranean Gull *1st-winter*

Black-headed Gull

7 Common Gull

1 Mediterranean Gull

4 Little Gull

Hilary Burn

Lesser Black-backed Gull *Larus fuscus*

Several thousand years ago, a successful species of gull which nested in the Northern Hemisphere started to expand its range both eastwards and westwards. As it colonised new areas, so new races developed and eventually different species evolved. Two of these species are found in the British Isles: the Herring Gull which is descended from birds which spread from the west, and the Lesser Black-back whose ancestors came from the east. These species are, therefore, closely related, and their behaviour is similar; but they rarely inter-breed.

Many Lesser Black-backs nest on or near the coast, but they also nest inland, often on high moorland.

Traditionally, Lesser Black-backs have been regarded as summer migrants, but in the last few years many, especially adults, have wintered in the British Isles.

Lesser Black-backs from Scandinavia also winter here and may be recognized by their much darker backs.

Herring Gull *Larus argentatus*

Most Herring Gulls do not look like adults until their fourth year. Although it takes a long time to become fully adult, a Herring Gull may have a long life: one individual is known to have lived 32 years.

Herring Gull colonies are mainly on cliffs, but they will also nest on rocky islands, dunes or shingle beaches and inland; recently some have started nesting on roofs of houses. The number of Herring Gulls has been increasing rapidly and because of their aggressive nature some have had to be killed in order to protect other species, such as terns, which nest nearby.

Herring Gulls feed on a wide range of food: they will follow fishing boats to pick up scraps, they eat eggs, small mammals, carrion and visit rubbish tips. They have learned to drop shellfish onto rocks in order to get at the contents.

When feeding young, the red spot on the adult's bill is important as chicks peck at red by instinct and this pecking prompts the parents to regurgitate food.

Glaucous Gull *Larus hyperboreus*

An increasing number of Glaucous Gulls are being seen in the British Isles. They are great scavengers and regularly visit harbours used by fishing boats and also rubbish tips. Some now summer in northern Scotland and have interbred with Herring Gulls in Shetland.

The rare Iceland Gull *Larus glaucoides* is also sometimes seen in winter.

Lesser Black-backed Gull
Smaller than Herring Gull – 55 cm. Also lighter build with longer legs. Wings are longer than Herring Gull's and appear narrower. Smaller than Great Black-backed with smaller head and bill. Adult (**1**) has dark grey or black back and yellow legs. Immatures (**2**) similar to immature Herring Gulls but have generally darker backs. *Breeds in colonies, usually near the coast. Some winter here.*

Herring Gull (3)
A large gull – 60 cm. Larger than Common Gull; has heavy, yellow bill with a red spot, and a fierce look. Back and upperwings are grey with white spots on the black tips. Legs are flesh-coloured or yellow. Immatures (**4**) generally have paler backs than Lesser Black-backs. *Nests all around our shores. Seen inland in winter.*

Glaucous Gull
Varies between Herring and Great Black-backed in size – 65–80 cm. Large head and bill. Adult (**5**) has pale grey back and white wing-tips. Immatures (**6**) are paler brown than other immature gulls with even paler wing-tips and no dark band on tail. *Mainly a winter visitor to east coast of Britain. Some summer in Shetland.*

Iceland Gull
Size of Herring Gull – 60 cm. Both adult (**7**) and juvenile are very similar to Glaucous, but smaller with a shorter, less heavy bill. *Winter visitor to east coast of Britain.*

4 Herring Gull *immature*

Herring Gull *immature*

6 Glaucous Gull *immature*

2 Lesser Black-backed Gull *immature*

3 Herring Gull

Herring Gulls

Great Black-backed Gull

Lesser Black-backed Gull *immature*

5 Glaucous Gull

7 Iceland Gull

Lesser Black-backed Gull *Scandinavian race*

1 Lesser Black-backed Gull

Hilary Burn

Great Black-backed Gull *Larus marinus*

The Great Black-backed Gull has been increasing in numbers during this century. Between 1930 and 1956, the number of breeding pairs trebled and the species continues to increase.

This fierce and predatory gull often feeds on other seabirds: Puffins and Manx Shearwaters are frequent victims. Great Black-backs also feed on carrion, fish, other birds' eggs, shellfish, and also rabbits which they catch and kill. They are often to be seen around fishing ports, where they feed on scraps; although less tame than Herring Gulls, away from man they will dominate other species in their efforts to get food.

Most pairs of Great Black-backs nest on or near the coast, but this species is often seen inland and, in recent years, greater numbers have roosted regularly on inland lakes and reservoirs in winter.

Kittiwake *Rissa tridactyla*

A truly coastal gull. No other member of this family is so dependent on the sea or spends so much time in the open ocean as the Kittiwake. They are at home far out to sea, where they find sufficient food, drink sea water and survive the fiercest winter gales. Kittiwakes often live for 20 years or more.

Nests, mainly consisting of seaweed, are built on small ledges on the steepest cliffs where eggs and young are safe from predators. Mammals cannot reach them and even larger gulls and skuas find it difficult to approach. These gulls always nest in colonies; the oldest ones usually return first in spring and generally nest in the centre of the colony; youngest birds return last and nest on the edges.

Juveniles leave their colonies in autumn and cross the Atlantic to the coast of Greenland where they join immatures from northern Europe, the USSR and more local birds from Newfoundland and Greenland. Our young Kittiwakes remain on the other side of the Atlantic for one or two years before returning to the colony of their birth. They will not breed until at least four years old.

The number of Kittiwakes has greatly increased during this century. One fascinating result of this increase has been the growth of colonies on buildings near the sea: ruined castles, warehouses and even seafront hotels now have Kittiwakes nesting on their window-sills and other convenient ledges.

Great Black-backed Gull
Larger than Lesser Black-back – 64–79 cm. A gull with large head and bill. Looks heavy in flight, wings appear broad and the body bulky. Adult (**1**) has black upperparts and pink legs. Immatures (**2**) are streaky grey-brown with bold 'chequered' pattern.
Breeds on rocky coasts and seen elsewhere outside the breeding season. Rarely in large numbers away from the coast.

Kittiwake
Smaller than Herring Gull – 41 cm. Rather like small Common Gull with slim, yellow bill, short black legs, and dark eye and slightly forked tail. Adult (**3**) has grey back and wings with jet black wing-tips. In winter (**4**) adults have smoky grey back to head. Juvenile (**5**) has black mark behind eye, black half-collar, black band on tail and black W pattern on wings. 1st-summer birds (**6**) are like juveniles, but dark marks are much faded. Name comes from the call: a noisy 'kitti-wa-ak'.
Nests on tiny ledges on steep sea cliffs or, occasionally, on buildings. Commonly seen around our coast, but rather unusual inland.

1 Great
Black-backed
Gulls

Great
Black-backed
Gull

2 Great
Black-backed
Gull
Immature

3 *adult summer*

5 *juveniles*
Kittiwakes

4 *adult winter*

5 *juvenile*

Kittiwakes

6 *1st-summer*

Hilary Burn.

Common Tern *Sterna hirundo*

It is not surprising that these graceful birds, with their long wings and forked tails, have been called 'sea-swallows'. Yet many nest miles from the sea, on inland shingle banks near rivers and around lakes or newly dug gravel or sand pits. Others are seen over land during their spring or autumn migration.

Common Terns may be seen in the British Isles between April and October. They fly south in autumn and most winter off the western African coast, as far south as South Africa.

Common Terns catch fish, insects and other prey by diving into the water. In coastal areas, the most commonly caught fish is the sand-eel. In spring birds fly over their territories carrying a fish and calling loudly. Later the fish may be presented by the male to the female.

Some colonies of Common Terns have become smaller in recent years because the best nest-sites have been taken over by gulls.

Arctic Tern *Sterna paradisaea*

No bird sees as much daylight in the course of a year as an Arctic Tern. It is truly a long-distance migrant, which breeds mainly north of the Arctic Circle and migrates in autumn to its winter feeding grounds on the very edge of Antarctica.

In the British Isles, the Arctic Tern is at the southern edge of its breeding range. Few pairs breed in southern England and Wales, but in Scotland Arctic Terns are numerous, especially around the coast, and greatly outnumber Common Terns.

As with other terns most of the food is caught below the water surface, by diving. When feeding, they will frequently hover. On their breeding grounds they will drive away intruders by swooping at them and pecking with the tip of their bill.

Identification of Common and Arctic Terns may be difficult, especially when mixed flocks of juveniles move along coasts in autumn; when not specifically identified, birdwatchers call them 'Commic Terns'!

Roseate Tern *Sterna dougallii*

The British Isles has the largest population of Roseate Terns in Europe, but even here the numbers have recently declined to only about 1,000 pairs. The growing number of gulls at Roseate Tern colonies is one serious problem; another is the trapping of these terns by small boys in West Africa.

Common Tern
Smaller than Black-headed Gull – 35 cm. Long, narrow, pointed wings and deeply forked tail. Adult in summer (1) has black cap and red bill with black tip. Best field mark is the dark outer primary feathers which appear as a dark wedge and contrast with the pale, translucent inner primaries. Adult in autumn (2) has white forehead, browner back and black bill. Call is a drawn-out 'kee-aarr'.
Summer visitor to coasts and inland lakes.

Arctic Tern
Size of Common Tern – 35 cm and very similar, but with slightly shorter legs, and rounder, smaller head. Adult (3) has all-red bill, white (not grey) rump, darker underparts, and lacks dark 'wedge' on wings. Juveniles (4) have pink base to black bill and more brown on back than juvenile Common Tern. Call 'kee-ar'.
Summer visitor, nesting around the coast mainly in the north. A few colonies inland.

Roseate Tern
Larger than Common Tern – 38 cm. Slender body and longer legs than Common. Adults (5) are whiter than Common or Arctic. Bill is black, often with a red base. In spring, breast is a rosy pink. Long tail streamers project beyond wings when perched. Call is rough 'aach aach'. Juvenile (6) has black legs, dark head and white edge to underside of wings.
Summer visitor nesting mainly on a few rocky or sandy islands.

2 Common Tern *autumn*

Arctic Tern *autumn*

4 Arctic Tern *juvenile*

Common Tern *juvenile*

Roseate Tern *autumn*

6 Roseate Tern *juvenile*

3 Arctic Tern

5 Roseate Tern

1 Common Tern

Hilary Burn

Sandwich Tern *Sterna sandvicensis*

This, the largest of Britain's breeding terns, no longer nests at Sandwich Bay in Kent, where it was first identified and named. These birds are, however, still regularly seen there on migration, and there are colonies in other parts of the British Isles, mostly on sand or shingle bars, or grass-covered islands. These colonies are easily disturbed and sometimes all the birds will leave if suddenly alarmed and not return again.

Some Sandwich Terns seem to prefer to nest near Black-headed Gulls. Although they sometimes lose their food to the more aggressive gulls they probably benefit from the protection given by the Black-headed Gulls, which chase away the larger predatory gulls.

Food is mainly small fish, which may be caught up to 20 km from the breeding colonies. While the adults are away fishing, the chicks often gather together in crèches which may help to protect the young, but just how the parents find their chicks again in a large moving flock is a real mystery.

Little Tern *Sterna albifrons*

Unfortunately for the Little Tern, it has a liking for many of the beaches which are used by holiday-makers, and each year many pairs fail to nest successfully because they are disturbed by humans. Little Tern protection schemes are now in operation in several parts of the country and the colonies, mostly small, are fenced. Collectors do, however, sometimes take eggs, and the tern's habit of nesting low down on beaches results in many nests being lost during storms or at high tides.

In other parts of the world, even as close as France, Little Terns nest inland along rivers, but in the British Isles they are found only around sea coasts, where they usually fish close to the shore.

Black Tern *Chlidonias niger*

Although Black Terns are regular visitors in spring and autumn, they ceased to breed here regularly in the middle of the last century.

Belonging to a family known as marsh terns, the Black Tern breeds mainly near fresh water. In the British Isles, it is most likely to be seen on migration, hunting over inland lakes and reservoirs, although it is frequently seen near the coasts as well. Its typical flight is rather buoyant, but it often dips down to pick insects or other food from the surface of the water.

Sandwich Tern
Larger than Black-headed Gull – 41 cm. Longer, narrower wings and less deeply forked tail than Common Tern. Bill is black with yellow tip. Adult (**1**) in summer has pale upperparts, black cap and untidy crest. Forehead is white in winter, but often starts to whiten during the summer. Juvenile (**2**) is like adult in winter, but browner with brown, spotted crown. Call is harsh 'kirrick'.
Summer visitor to sea coasts. Rare inland.

Little Tern
Smaller than Black-headed Gull – 24 cm. Smallest sea-tern. Adult in summer (**3**) has yellow bill with black tip, yellow legs, black cap with white forehead, dark line through eye and dark outer flight feathers. Juvenile (**4**) has darker bill and brown marks on back and head. Flight is hurried and bird often hovers. Call is 'kik-kik'.
Summer visitor to sandy or shingle beaches.

Black Tern
Smaller than Black-headed Gull – 24 cm. Slightly forked tail and graceful flight. Adult in summer (**5**) has black head and body with grey wings and white under the tail. In autumn (**6**) has white head, neck and body with dark crown and white neck-collar with dark mark on shoulders. Juvenile is like autumn adult. Call 'kik, kik'. Often dips down to pick food from the water surface.
Very rare breeding bird, seen mainly in spring and autumn.

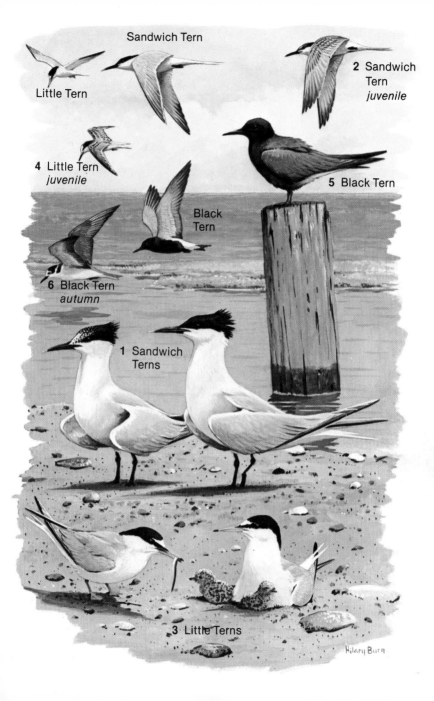

Sandwich Tern

Little Tern

2 Sandwich Tern *juvenile*

4 Little Tern *juvenile*

Black Tern

5 Black Tern

6 Black Tern *autumn*

1 Sandwich Terns

3 Little Terns

Hilary Burn

Guillemot *Uria aalge*

This is our most numerous seabird and the drama of its large, noisy, and often smelly northern colonies must be seen to be appreciated. The birds breed where the sea cliffs are steepest, and crowd together on tiny ledges or on flat-topped stacks. The single egg, which is incubated between the bird's feet, is pear-shaped and spins if knocked, so it is therefore less likely to roll off a cliff-edge.

The southern race of Guillemots has a browner back and head than the northern race which is similar in colour to a Razorbill. The form of Guillemot known as 'bridled' becomes more numerous towards the Arctic; in the south of Britain, only 1% of Guillemots are bridled compared with about 26% in Shetland.

Guillemots leave their colonies when the young are only half grown and all disappear out to sea, away from the large, predatory gulls. Most adults will winter in British or Irish waters, although the young may travel farther afield. Many become victims of oil pollution incidents and are frequently washed ashore dead or dying.

Razorbill *Alca torda*

The British Isles are important as the breeding ground for many seabirds, especially the Razorbill: about 70% of its world population breeds here. Although not so numerous as Guillemots, Razorbills are rather more widespread. They nest among fallen boulders or in crevices and prefer sites where a rock roof gives their eggs and chicks some protection from gulls.

Razorbills' eggs are not pear-shaped like those of the Guillemot, but a more oval shape, as they are not normally laid on narrow ledges and are less likely to be knocked into the sea.

Young leave the cliffs when half grown. First- and second-year birds are migratory and may winter in the Bay of Biscay, while some even reach the Mediterranean. Older birds remain closer to the British Isles and, like Guillemots, suffer from oil pollution incidents.

Little Auk *Alle alle*

This, our smallest auk, is usually seen only when strong winds force it near our coasts, or even, occasionally, inland.

Little Auks feed on plankton and nest in the Arctic. Some of their breeding colonies contain more than a million pairs and the droppings below the colony help lush vegetation to grow, which is then grazed on by geese and reindeer.

Guillemot (1)
Larger than Jackdaw – 42 cm. Dark brown-and-white penguin-like bird with black pointed bill. Some, known as bridled Guillemots (2), have white 'spectacle' markings. Flight is fast with rapid wingbeats. In winter (3), neck and sides of head are white. Call is a growling 'arrr'.
Breeds on rocky coasts. In winter is seen mainly out to sea.

Razorbill (4)
Slightly smaller than Guillemot – 41 cm. Head and upperparts are black. Bill is black, deep and has white marks. When swimming, appears more plump than Guillemot, and its longer, more pointed tail is raised. In winter (5) has white neck and cheeks. 1st-winter birds have smaller bills.
Breeds on remote cliffs, stacks and rocky islands.

Little Auk
Size of Starling – 21 cm. Dumpy and short necked. Black-and-white in summer with a short, stubby bill. In winter (6) has white sides to neck and white throat and cheeks. Flies with fast wingbeats, and wings hardly raised above the level of the body. Underwing pattern is variable, but often appears dark.
Mainly a winter visitor, usually seen when storms at sea force it close to the shore.

Razorbill

Guillemot

4 Razorbills

6 Little Auks
winter

3 Guillemots
winter

1 Guillemots

5 Razorbill
winter

2 Guillemot
bridled

Hilary Burn

Black Guillemot *Cepphus grylle*

Known also by its old Viking name of 'Tystie', the Black Guillemot is by far the rarest of our breeding auks. Like other members of the family, it needs rocky coasts for nesting, but not open cliff ledges like the Guillemot; instead, it nests in holes, crevices, under boulders and, often, in caves. Occasionally, young are reared in man-made structures such as holes in harbour walls or ruined buildings.

Before the breeding season gets underway, adults may be seen displaying: chasing, diving and calling with beaks open, showing their bright red mouths.

The chief food is fish, which is caught during dives lasting a minute or more and often taking place closer to the shore than those of other auks. They do not migrate far from their breeding grounds in winter and even those which breed in the Arctic may move only to the nearest ice-free water, where their pale winter plumage gives them the advantage of camouflage.

Puffin *Fratercula arctica*

The Puffin is familiar to most people, yet it nests mainly on remote islands and can be very difficult to observe. The populations fluctuate: recently the numbers breeding at some northern colonies have shown remarkable increases but those colonies in the extreme south of the species' range have declined.

Some Puffins breed in holes in cliff-faces or among boulders, but most nest in burrows on the grassy cliff-tops. The burrows are either dug out by the Puffins themselves or taken over from rabbits. The main enemies of nesting Puffins are rats and the large gulls; the safest colonies are on 'rat-free' islands or on steep slopes where gulls have more difficulty in attacking.

When feeding young, Puffins may be seen carrying ten or more fish in their bill. They can open their bills so that the two halves are parallel, and this, together with a series of hooks inside the bill, helps them to hold one fish while catching another. Fishing Puffins probably zig-zag through shoals of fish which helps to explain why their prey is usually arranged alternately head-to-tail when carried in the bill.

Only one egg is laid, and the solitary chick remains in the burrow for six weeks, until fully grown, at which point the parents stop feeding it. A week later, it leaves the burrow and makes its way to the sea. This first journey usually takes place at night, but gulls and skuas still manage to kill many young Puffins before they reach the sea.

Black Guillemot
Size of Jackdaw – 34 cm. In summer (**1**) is black with large white wing-patches. Legs and feet are bright red. In winter (**2**) is largely white with mottled back. Juveniles are like adults in winter, but browner. Frequently dives.
Breeds on rocky coasts mainly in northern and western Britain and all around the coast of Ireland.

Puffin
Smaller than feral Rock Dove – 30 cm. Black-and-white with colourful, triangular bill in summer (**3**), clown-like face and red feet. In winter (**4**) face of adult is dusky and bill is less colourful. Juvenile (**5**) has small dark bill and dusky cheeks. Call is a growling 'arrr'.
Breeds in burrows on cliff-tops, mostly on islands. Winters at sea.

Puffins

Black
Guillemots

1 Black Guillemots

Guillemot
winter

Razorbill
winter

4 Puffin
winter

2 Black Guillemot
winter

5 Puffin
juvenile

3 Puffin

Hilary Burn.

Rock Dove *Columba livia*

Truly wild Rock Doves are at home only on the rocky, windswept coasts of western Scotland and Ireland. They feed mainly on seeds, and nest and roost on cliff ledges or in caves. It is from these birds that our familiar 'town pigeon' is descended.

For thousands of years, these birds have been domesticated. Special dovecotes have been built to provide safe roosts and nest-sites so that the young pigeons could be killed to provide fresh meat, especially in winter.

Many pigeons ignored their specially built homes and moved into town and city centres where they were safe from predators and found suitable nest-sites on the surrounding buildings. To these urban flocks came colourful 'fancy' pigeons which had escaped, and also lost 'homing pigeons'. Now the variety of plumage colours is bewildering, but many still retain very similar colours to their Rock Dove ancestors.

So widespread are feral Rock Doves that it is possible that there are only a few pure Rock Doves left wild in the British Isles. Some of the feral birds have also returned to their original nest-sites on cliff ledges around our coasts.

Stock Dove *Columba oenas*

These birds are the only pigeons or doves in the British Isles which regularly nest in holes in trees. They may be found in a wide range of different habitats from large gardens to rocky cliffs. They nest wherever there are old trees, but will also nest in holes in buildings or on cliffs, under bushes or even in burrows.

Early in the last century, Stock Doves were found only in southeastern England, but then they spread to many new areas. In the 1950s, they started to decline, but are now increasing again.

In spite of liking town parks, Stock Doves rarely feed with feral Rock Doves; instead, they feed mainly on grain and other seeds. Flocks of Stock Doves may often be seen feeding together, sometimes with Woodpigeons.

Look out for breeding Stock Doves displaying in spring or summer. In their aerial display, they fly in large circles with wings held in a shallow V. On the ground, the male puffs out his neck feathers and calls while bowing to the female.

Rock Dove
33 cm. Blue-grey, with paler grey back, white rump, two black wing-bars and white underwing. The familiar feral Rock Dove (**1**) has a variety of plumages, including dark grey, reddish-brown and white. Some resemble true wild Rock Doves.
True Rock Doves are only found on remote, rocky, western coasts of Scotland and Ireland. Feral Rock Doves are common in towns throughout the British Isles.

Stock Dove (2)
Size of Rock Dove – 33 cm. Smaller and darker than Woodpigeon without white patches on wings or neck. Has two short black wing-bars and black rear edge to wings. Differs from Rock Dove by having grey rump. Call is rather deep, quiet but far-carrying 'ooo-woo'.
Nests in woods, parks and farmland where there are old trees. Resident, found in most parts of the British Isles except the far north.

Stock Dove

Rock Doves
feral

1 Rock Doves
feral

Woodpigeon

2 Stock Dove

H. Tarry Burn.

Woodpigeon *Columba palumbus*

Once, Woodpigeons were numerous only in deciduous woods, but times have changed, and now they nest in town centres, in small copses, in hedges or even on the ground. In many areas, they are serious farmland pests.

One reason for their success is their long breeding season, which lasts from April to October, with some nesting in winter. Generally, Woodpigeons in towns nest earlier than those in farmland, many of which are rearing young at harvest time when there is a plentiful supply of grain. Apart from man, Woodpigeons have few enemies, which may also account for their success.

In summer their aerial display-flights may be seen, as they rise slowly, make a clapping sound with their wings and then glide down again. When alarmed, they crash out of a tree or bush and clap their wings loudly.

Woodpigeons eat mainly vegetable matter and they feed their young (called squabs) on a special fluid known as pigeon's milk which is made in the adult's crop.

Collared Dove *Streptopelia decaocto*

The Collared Dove is a newcomer to the British Isles. Its spread across Europe is a remarkable story. At the start of this century, it was found only in Asia and southeast Europe. Then, in about 1930, it began to spread north-westwards, reaching Austria in 1938 and the Netherlands in 1947.

The first Collared Doves to breed in Britain nested in Norfolk in 1955, and the species has now spread to the west coast of Ireland and Shetland, and has even reached Iceland.

Although Collared Doves lay a clutch of only two eggs, their breeding season may last from March to September and up to five broods may be reared in one year. This fast breeding and lack of competition with other species has helped their extraordinary increase in numbers.

Turtle Dove *Streptopelia turtur*

The Turtle Dove is the only pigeon or dove which is a summer visitor to Britain and Ireland. It returns from its winter quarters in West Africa in late April or May, and its soothing, purring song is to be heard in the English countryside for most of the summer.

Like other pigeons, Turtle Doves are largely vegetarian, feeding on seeds of many plants especially fumitory. Their flimsy nests are built in tall bushes or hedges and two eggs are laid. Two broods are usually reared before the doves leave again in late summer.

Woodpigeon (1)
Larger than Rock Dove – 41 cm. Largest dove or pigeon. Plump, with rather small head. White patch on side of neck and white bars across wings. Pinkish breast and dark band on tail. Juvenile (2) lacks white on sides of neck. Song is a soothing 'co-coo-coo, coo-co'. Often seen in large flocks, especially in winter.
Found in woods, farmland and town parks, throughout the British Isles except some northern islands.

Collared Dove (3)
Slightly smaller than Rock Dove – 32 cm. Rather long tail, dark wing-tips and black half-collar. Plumage is pinkish-grey. White outer tail feathers when seen from above, distinct black-and-white tail pattern when seen from below. Song is monotonous 'co-cooo-cok'.
Widespread in the British Isles, usually near towns, villages or farms.

Turtle Dove (4)
Slightly smaller than Rock Dove – 32 cm. Small, slim dove. Generally darker than Collared Dove with 'scaly' back and black-and-white patch on neck. Tail is black with white border. Call is a loud purring noise. Flight is often very rapid.
Summer migrant to woods and farmland in south and east Britain. Rare in Scotland and Ireland.

Woodpigeon *display*

Turtle Dove

Collared Dove

Woodpigeon

Stock Dove

Turtle Dove

3 Collared Dove

Collared Dove

2 Woodpigeon *juvenile*

4 Turtle Dove

1 Woodpigeon

Hilary Burn

Ring-necked Parakeet *Psittacula krameri*

The Ring-necked Parakeet is common in India and parts of Africa and many have been brought to Britain as cage birds. Some have escaped or been deliberately released and are now breeding wild in parts of England. They have survived cold winters and are showing signs of increasing and spreading to new areas.

They nest in holes in trees and feed on buds and fruit. They will also visit bird tables in winter. If numbers continue to increase, it is likely that this species may become a serious nuisance to fruit farmers.

Cuckoo *Cuculus canorus*

There are few life histories so strange as that of the Cuckoo. It spends the winter in central or even southern Africa and returns to the British Isles in April, when its familiar song is usually welcomed as a sign of spring. It feeds mainly on insects and their larvae, especially hairy caterpillars which are not usually eaten by birds.

While Cuckoos are pairing and claiming territories, noisy chases take place as males pursue females. Later, the male's display may be seen as he bobs and sways on a perch with wings drooped and tail raised and spread.

A female will usually return to the area where she was reared and there she will search out nests of small insectivorous birds, such as Dunnock, Meadow Pipit, Wren or Reed Warbler. She will wait until a nest contains some eggs and then lays her own eggs in it. After laying, she will remove one of the other eggs and then leave the host species to incubate her egg. The young Cuckoo generally hatches first and, although blind and unfeathered, instinctively sets about the task of pushing out the other eggs so that it will have the sole attention of its foster parents.

Eggs of Cuckoos may resemble those of the host species. The female cannot change the colour of her eggs, but she usually chooses one particular species, often the one by which she was reared and which her eggs sometimes, but not always, match.

Adult Cuckoos leave the British Isles in July and early August, but the young birds do not leave until late August or September.

Ring-necked Parakeet
Size of Woodpigeon – 41 cm. Bright green with very long tail and red bill. Male (1) has thin black line running from bill around his neck. Regularly makes loud screech in flight. *Resident in parts of England and is spreading to new areas, often on the edge of towns.*

Cuckoo (2)
Slightly smaller than Kestrel – 33 cm. Rather like male Sparrowhawk with long tail, grey upperparts and barred underparts, but wings are pointed and the tail is graduated and spotted with white. Juvenile (3) is generally reddish-brown and rather Kestrel-like; it has a white spot on the back of its head. Flight is hawk-like with shallow wingbeats. Song is well-known 'cuckoo', but other sounds are made, including a bubbling call by the female. *Summer visitor to most parts of the British Isles.*

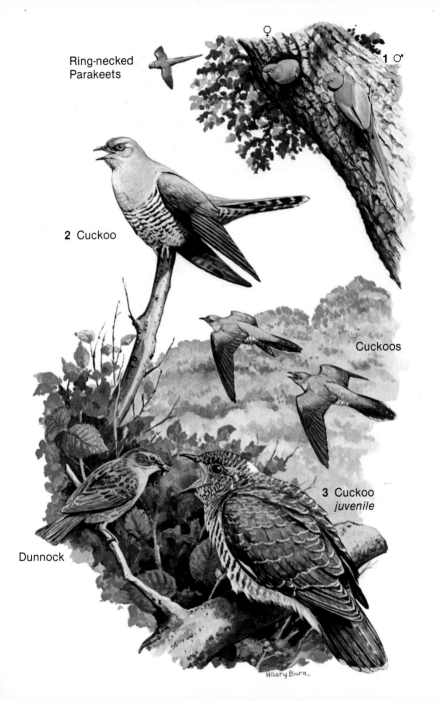

Ring-necked
Parakeets

♀

1 ♂

2 Cuckoo

Cuckoos

Dunnock

3 Cuckoo *juvenile*

Hilary Burn.

Barn Owl *Tyto alba*

This species hunts mainly at night, but may sometimes be seen hunting in daylight in winter, when food is in short supply, or in summer when feeding young.

Although many Barn Owls nest in barns, others use holes in old trees. Unfortunately, modern barns are not as suitable for nesting Barn Owls as old ones, some of which even had special holes to allow owls easy access.

The Barn Owl population has declined. Loss of suitable habitat caused by changing farming methods and the use of toxic chemicals are thought to have been responsible. They should be welcomed on farms as rats, mice and shrews make up 90% of their prey.

Barn Owls rely on their superb hearing to locate their prey and they hunt by flying close to the ground with a slow wavering flight and sometimes hovering.

The Snowy Owl *Nyctea scandiaca* is a very large, mainly white owl which sometimes visits northern Britain from the Arctic. It has nested in Shetland.

Tawny Owl *Strix aluco*

This is the commonest owl in Britain (but is absent from Ireland). It may be found even in towns, provided that there are old trees in which it can roost and nest. Usually it nests in a hole in a tree, but will also use old buildings, holes in cliffs or even disused nests of larger birds such as crows.

Tawnys usually hunt at night. By day, they roost in holes or in trees, close to the trunk, where they may be 'mobbed' by small birds which give alarm calls to draw attention to the predator.

When hunting, they often use a perch from which they drop onto their prey. They feed mainly on small mammals and birds, but insects and worms are also taken.

Little Owl *Athene noctua*

This owl is widespread throughout Europe, but did not breed in Britain until the end of the last century, when there were several attempts to introduce it into various parts of England. Some of these attempts were successful and now the Little Owl is quite common on lowland farms and in many other habitats, including towns. It does not, however, breed in Ireland.

Little Owls may often be seen in daylight, sitting on road-side walls or posts. Much of their hunting takes place at dawn or dusk. The chief prey consists of insects, worms, mammals and small birds.

A hole in a deciduous tree is the most common nest-site; some have been in use for at least 25 years.

Barn Owl (1)
Smaller than Woodpigeon – 34 cm. White underparts and honey-coloured back with dark marks. White face is rather monkey-like. Makes a long, eerie shriek as well as other 'hissing' or 'snoring' calls.
Found mainly on farmland in most parts of Britain and Ireland. Rarer in northern Scotland.

Tawny Owl (2)
Smaller than Woodpigeon – 38 cm. Large brown owl with darker marks and white flecks on its back. Underparts are pale with dark streaks. Wings are broad and rounded. Tail is short. Song is the familiar 'hoohoo-oo-oooo' and a loud, sharp 'kewick'.
Lives in woods throughout Britain. Not found in Ireland.

Little Owl (3)
Size of Starling – 22 cm. Small and flat-headed. Brown back is spotted with white. Underparts are pale with brown streaks. Bobs when alarmed. Flight is undulating, usually close to the ground. Has repetitive 'kiew-kiew' call, rather like a mewing kitten.
Found mainly on farmland and in parkland in England and Wales.

2 Tawny Owl

Barn Owl

3 Little Owls

1 Barn Owl

Hilary Burn

Long-eared Owl *Asio otus*

In Britain, the Long-eared Owl breeds mainly in conifer woodland or in pine trees in isolated plantations. In Ireland, where it is the commonest owl, it is as likely to be found in deciduous as in coniferous woods. It often breeds in old nests of other species, especially those of Magpie, Carrion Crow or Sparrowhawk.

Long-eared Owls hunt mainly at night and feed on small mammals, birds and insects. Although most are resident, others arrive here from northern Europe for the winter, and communal roosts of 12 or more of these owls may sometimes be found. In some winters, exceptionally high numbers are seen.

The tufts of feathers on the head are, of course, not ears, but probably used by the owls to communicate. They are raised when nervous, but always lie flat in flight.

Short-eared Owl *Asio flammeus*

A hunting Short-eared Owl flies one or two metres from the ground, flapping, gliding and sometimes hovering as it searches for short-tailed voles which make up 65% of its diet. Other small mammals and birds are also caught. Much of the hunting takes place during daylight.

As with many birds of prey, incubation begins as soon as the first egg is laid, so the young hatch at intervals. When food is scarce, only the eldest and strongest will live, but, when food is plentiful, the whole brood may survive. The population of these owls depends, therefore, on the population of voles.

In winter, these owls may visit farmland, rough ground and coastal marshes. Numbers appear to be increasing, perhaps because there are now many young conifer plantations which provide ideal nest-sites.

Nightjar *Caprimulgus europaeus*

At dusk, most insect-eating birds go to roost, but it is then that the Nightjar becomes active: twisting and turning in flight as it catches night-flying insects, especially moths, in its large mouth. On summer evenings, the strange, continuous, almost mechanical song may be heard, the pitch altering as the bird turns its head.

Nightjars winter in Africa and are one of the last migrants to return here in spring. During the day, they perch lengthways on a branch and are beautifully camouflaged. They nest on the ground where, again, they blend with their surroundings.

During this century, Nightjars have declined. Fewer pairs rear two broods, apparently as a result of cold springs and wet autumns, which give shorter summers.

Long-eared Owl (1)
Slightly smaller than Tawny Owl – 36 cm, with longer wings and tail. Rather slender, with delicately streaked body, cat-like face and orange eyes. Ear-tufts show only when perched. In flight, it has deep wingbeats followed by a glide with wings held in line with the body; the underparts show up as uniformly dark. Song is a low, drawn-out hoot. Young give high-pitched squeaks, like an unoiled hinge.
A secretive owl of woods in many parts of Britain and Ireland.

Short-eared Owl (2)
Size of Tawny Owl – 38 cm. Long wings and short tail. Mottled brown upperparts. Streaked breast, but pale belly and flanks. Round face and fierce yellow eyes. Often perches on the ground. When hunting, flies low with a few wingbeats followed by a glide with wings held in shallow V. Call a hoarse bark. Song a hollow 'boo-boo-boo-boo'.
Breeds in open country, especially moorland and young plantations in northern Britain. More widespread in winter.

Nightjar
Smaller than Kestrel – 27 cm. Long tail and long wings. Silent, hawk-like flight. Delicately marked grey-and-brown plumage. Male (3) has white spots on wings and tail. Loud churring song is made after dark. Flight call is sharp 'coo-ik'. Wings are clapped in display.
Summer visitor to heaths, moors and plantations, mainly in the south.

Long-eared Owl

Short-eared Owl

3 Nightjar ♂

Nightjar

1 Long-eared Owl

2 Short-eared Owl

Hilary Burn.

Swift *Apus apus*

When a young Swift leaves its nest, it may not land again for months or even years! Swifts are perfectly adapted to life on the wing: they sleep, eat, drink, gather nest material and even mate without landing.

Within a few days of leaving its nest in a hole in a building, or a crack in a cliff-face, the young Swift will be heading for central or southeastern Africa, where it will spend the winter before returning the following spring. Not until its fourth year will it be able to breed successfully. Some immature Swifts may remain in Africa for a whole summer; others will travel north, but roam over Europe.

Swifts have all four of their toes pointing forwards which helps them to cling to vertical surfaces. They do not usually land on the ground deliberately and, if they do so, they may have difficulty in becoming airborne again.

Hoopoe *Upupa epops*

This exotic bird is a rather rare visitor to the British Isles, but each spring a few appear to overshoot their normal breeding areas in central and southern Europe and arrive in Britain or Ireland, mainly near the south or east coasts. Very occasionally a pair will stay and breed.

The bird's name comes from its curious whooping call, made with its head between its legs. It feeds mainly on insect larvae and often feeds on areas of short grass, where it probes with its long bill.

Kingfisher *Alcedo atthis*

A Kingfisher usually hunts from a branch, or some other perch, overhanging a stream or river, but will also sometimes hover before plunging into the water to seize an unsuspecting fish. A variety of small fish are caught, including sticklebacks and bullheads which have to be beaten against a branch before being swallowed, head first.

Kingfishers lay their eggs in a chamber at the end of a tunnel, dug into a river bank or some other soft cliff. Nests become very smelly and unpleasant while in use.

The iridescent blue of the Kingfisher is not a true colour, but is caused by light being reflected off the microscopic parts of the feathers; this is known as 'structural colour'.

Kingfishers are usually found near slow-flowing rivers or lakes. Some remain all winter so long as waters remain unfrozen, but others move downstream and visit coastal waters. In cold winters, many die. Water pollution also seriously affects Kingfisher populations and may have eliminated this species from some industrial areas.

Swift (1)
16.5 cm. Shorter body, but longer wings than Swallow. Dark brown, with pale throat, short forked tail and narrow, crescent-shaped wings. Never perches on wires and rarely lands. Flight is fast and call is a shrill screech. Often seen in flocks. Juveniles have a 'scaly' appearance.
Summer visitor from May to August. Seen in town and country in most of the British Isles.

Hoopoe (2)
Smaller than Rock Dove – 28 cm. Long, downcurved bill; pinkish-brown plumage; broad, rounded, black-and-white wings and a large crest which may be raised or lowered. Has curious bouncing flight. Song is quiet but far-carrying 'oop-oop-oop'.
Unusual spring migrant and summer visitor, seen mainly in southern England.

Kingfisher
A little larger than House Sparrow – 16.5 cm. Large head and bill, short tail. Bright blue-green upperparts with vivid blue streak on back. Underparts are chestnut. White throat and white patch on neck. Female (3) has red base to lower mandible. Call is a shrill whistle. Flight is fast, straight and, usually, low over water or nearby fields.
Found near lakes and rivers in England, Wales and Ireland, but only in a few places in southern Scotland.

1 Swifts

House Martin

Swallow

2 Hoopoes

3 Kingfisher
♀

Wryneck *Jynx torquilla*

Formerly, the Wryneck nested in holes in old trees, especially in orchards, in southeast England, but probably no longer does so. A few pairs have, however, recently started to breed in Scotland.

The name Wryneck comes from the way the bird twists and turns its head.

Green Woodpecker *Picus viridis*

The Green Woodpecker often feeds on the ground, where it hunts for ants and may, sometimes, be found a long way from any trees. On the ground, it appears clumsy and moves with a series of hops. If disturbed, the bright yellow rump is the most obvious feature as it flies away. Sometimes its distinctive droppings may be found: they resemble ash from a cigarette and contain the remains of hundreds of ants.

This woodpecker seldom 'drums', so the laughing call is the best clue that the species is in the area.

The nest-hole is excavated by both sexes and has an entrance 6.5 cm across. As with other woodpeckers, no nest material is used except for a few wood chips. In later years, woodpecker holes are valuable nest-sites for other hole-nesting birds, such as Starlings and tits.

Great Spotted Woodpecker *Dendrocopos major*

As with other woodpeckers, its flight is deeply undulating with wings almost closing at regular intervals. All woodpeckers climb trees in a series of hops with the stiff tail feathers pressed against the trunk for support.

A Great Spotted Woodpecker is seldom seen on the ground. It feeds on insects, nuts, seeds and berries.

Lesser Spotted Woodpecker *Dendrocopos minor*

This, our smallest woodpecker, is secretive and generally hard to observe. In spring, its call and drumming reveal its whereabouts. Drumming involves as many as 14–15 blows per second with the bill and its purpose is to declare territory, not to drill a nest-hole. The male has a wonderful moth-like display, but luck as well as patience are needed to observe it.

The nest-hole is excavated slowly in decaying wood, from one to as much as 20 m above ground, often on the underside of a branch.

The chief food of this woodpecker is wood-boring insects which are caught with its long tongue.

Wryneck (1)
Slightly larger than House Sparrow – 16.5 cm. Delicately marked brown plumage with darker brown, arrow-shaped mark on back. Rather short, pointed bill. *Rare breeding species in areas with old trees. More likely to be seen on migration, especially on the English east coast in spring or autumn.*

Green Woodpecker (2)
Size of feral Rock Dove – 32 cm. Largest British woodpecker. Dark green back, paler green below. Bright yellowish rump. Flight is undulating. Red crown. Juvenile (3) is heavily streaked. Loud laughing call. *Prefers parkland or other grassy areas with plenty of old trees. Widespread in the south and increasing in Scotland. Absent from Ireland.*

Great Spotted Woodpecker
Smaller than Blackbird – 23 cm. Large white patches on shoulders show well in flight. Male (4) has red nape: both sexes have red under the tail. Juvenile (5) has red crown. Call is loud 'tchick'. Flight is undulating. Loud drumming made in spring. *Found in most British woods, but not in Ireland.*

Lesser Spotted Woodpecker
Size of House Sparrow – 14 cm. Barred back and wings. Male (6) has red crown. Female (7) pale crown. Flight is undulating. Call is quiet 'tchick'. Song is high, fast 'pee-pee-pee'. Drumming is higher-pitched and longer than Great Spotted's. *Found in woodland and parkland in southern England and Wales.*

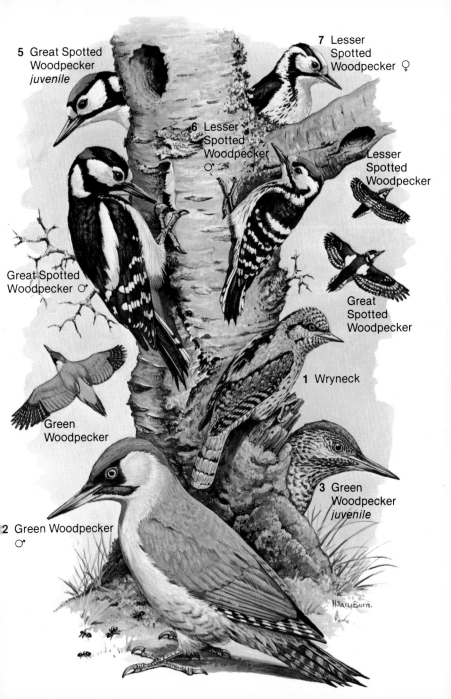

5 Great Spotted
Woodpecker
juvenile

7 Lesser
Spotted
Woodpecker ♀

6 Lesser
Spotted
Woodpecker
♂

Lesser
Spotted
Woodpecker

Great Spotted
Woodpecker ♂

Great
Spotted
Woodpecker

1 Wryneck

Green
Woodpecker

3 Green
Woodpecker
juvenile

2 Green Woodpecker
♂

Hilary Burn.

Woodlark *Lullula arborea*

In summer, Woodlarks are usually found on dry heath-land or downland where there are scattered trees which can be used as song-posts, long grass for nesting, and short grass for feeding. They also nest in recently cleared areas of woodland.

They are less likely to be seen in large flocks than are Skylarks, and they roam away from their breeding areas in winter. The number of Woodlarks breeding in Britain has decreased this century.

Skylark *Alauda arvensis*

The Skylark is the most widespread of any bird breeding in Britain or Ireland. Not only is it found on all types of farmland, but also on salt marshes, dunes and rough ground, and even in built-up areas. It is missing only from the tops of the highest mountains.

Song is important for declaring territory, and as Skylarks often breed in flat, treeless country they over-come the lack of song-posts by singing in the air, at a great height, over their nesting areas.

Our Skylarks are mostly resident, but in winter, especially in very cold weather, many more cross the North Sea and spend the winter here. In prolonged cold spells, a large proportion of Skylarks may die, but their numbers recover quickly after one or two good breeding seasons.

Skylarks feed on seeds, leaves, worms and insects and their larvae, as well as a variety of other animal and vegetable foods.

In the past, many were trapped and killed for food, their tongues being considered a great delicacy. Although trapping has now died out in the British Isles, it continues in some European countries, where vast numbers of Skylarks are killed each year.

Shore Lark *Eremophila alpestris*

For years, Shore Larks were rare winter visitors, but then numbers increased and a few remained in Scotland in summer. Breeding was suspected, and then proved in 1977.

Shore Larks normally nest on dry Arctic tundra, but also on more southerly short grassland in North America, in mountain ranges in North Africa and the Middle East and on upland steppes in central Asia.

Shore Larks nest on the ground, amongst vegetation. The young leave the nest before being able to fly; they split up and lie still when danger threatens, behaviour which helps to protect them from predators.

Woodlark (1)
Slightly larger than House Sparrow – 15 cm. Like Skylark, but smaller, with stripes over eyes which meet on back of head. Short tail has white corners. Black-and-white patch on leading edge of wing. Flight is rather jerky. Song is sweet and musical, given from a perch or in a circling song flight. Call is a pleasant 'kit loo-eet'.
Breeds mainly on heathland in southern England and parts of Wales.

Skylark (2)
Smaller than Starling – 18 cm. Brown streaked back, pale underparts and streaked breast. Short crest. Broad wings with pale hind edge. White outer tail feathers. Often seen in flocks in winter. Loud, clear, rapid, warbling song is usually given in a song flight as the bird rises, circles, hovers and then drifts downwards; also from posts or the ground.
Widespread throughout the British Isles.

Shore Lark
Smaller than Skylark – 16.5 cm. Pale brown upperparts, whitish below. Male (3) has yellow face with black on forehead, cheeks and breast, and also has two small black horns. Female, juvenile (4) and male in winter (5) have less distinct face markings.
Winter visitor, mainly seen on east coast of England. Has occasionally nested in Scotland.

Woodlark

Skylark

3 Shore Larks

♂

Shore Lark
♂ *winter*

Meadow
Pipit

2 Skylarks

4 Shore Lark
juvenile

Woodlark
juvenile

1 Woodlark

Hilary Burn.

Sand Martin *Riparia riparia*

This species returns to the British Isles in March, usually a few days, or even weeks, before the first Swallows. They winter in Africa, south of the Sahara, and most return to the same colony as the previous year.

Sand Martins nest in burrows which they usually dig for themselves in banks. Although some may tunnel in river banks or sea cliffs, many others use man-made cliffs in sand or gravel quarries.

Although Sand Martins are widespread, their numbers have declined in recent years, perhaps because of drought in their winter quarters or because of poor weather during the breeding season.

In autumn, large evening roosts of Sand Martins may gather in reedbeds, before the birds migrate.

Swallow *Hirundo rustica*

Once, long ago, it was thought that when Swallows disappeared in winter they hid at the bottom of lakes or flew to the moon. We know now that most of our Swallows fly to South Africa.

Most Swallows return here in April and rear two, and sometimes three, broods before migrating in the autumn. In the past, most Swallows must have nested in hollow trees or in caves; now, most nest inside buildings, especially barns, where their mud cup is built on a rafter or some other support.

Swallows hunt insects in the air. Their short, wide bills make it easier for them to catch their flying prey. Often they hunt over lakes and rivers where flying insects are more plentiful. Since they can feed while flying, martins and swallows can migrate in the daytime, whereas most other small birds migrate only at night.

House Martin *Delichon urbica*

Although House Martins are familiar summer visitors, their winter quarters are still undiscovered. We know they reach Africa, but exactly where they go in that vast continent remains a mystery.

House Martins once nested mainly on cliffs and some still do so; most, however, build cup-shaped nests under the eaves of houses. Nests may take 12–14 days to build and contain about 2,500 tiny pellets of mud. The birds prefer to nest in colonies and each pair may raise two or three broods each year. Young birds from early broods help to feed those in later broods.

Recently, House Martins have recolonised some city centres because more insects are now available as a result of cleaner air.

Sand Martin (1)
Smaller than Swallow – 12 cm. Brown back, white underparts and brown breast band. Fluttering flight is less graceful than Swallow's. Wings are pointed and tail slightly forked. Has chattering song and call. Often seen in parties.
Summer visitor. May be seen feeding over water in most parts of the British Isles.

Swallow
19 cm. Long, pointed wings, and forked tail with long streamers. Upperparts blue-black, underparts whitish, and face dark red. Juvenile (2) has slightly forked tail and no streamers. Male (3) usually has longer tail-streamers than female (4). Flight is graceful, often close to the ground. Call is rather sharp 'tswit'; also has twittering song.
Summer visitor to most of Britain and Ireland except for town centres, rugged mountains and remote islands.

House Martin (5)
Smaller than Swallow – 12.5 cm. Dark blue-black back, white underparts and white rump. Tail is forked. Rather fluttering flight on stiff, almost triangular wings. Call is 'chirrup'.
Summer visitor. Nests on buildings throughout Britain and Ireland. Rather scarce in northern Scotland.

Sand Martin
juvenile

Sand Martin

House
Martin

3 Swallow ♂

House
Martin

2 Swallow
juvenile

4 Swallow ♀

Swift

1 Sand
Martin

5 House
Martin

Swallow

Hilary Burn

Tree Pipit *Anthus trivialis*

Usually it is the song or call which first attracts one's attention to this small brown bird. Although a short version of the song may be given from a perch, the full song is heard only during the Tree Pipit's distinctive display flight, as the bird flutters steeply upwards, starts singing before it reaches maximum height and continues as it parachutes down, with wings raised and tail spread, to land on the perch from which it started, or at least close by.

Tree Pipits feed mainly on invertebrates which live on the ground, such as grasshoppers, beetles and spiders. They nest on the ground.

Meadow Pipit *Anthus pratensis*

Walk across a moorland in summer and it is quite possible that the only birds you will see will be Meadow Pipits; certainly they will outnumber any other species. Between March and July, their song flight may easily be seen as they rise from the ground with rather feeble notes gathering speed, followed by a succession of sweeter notes as they parachute down again. The advantages of this method of stating territory are obvious on moorland where there are few natural perches: an aerial display is by far the best method.

The Meadow Pipit is only a winter visitor to many lowland areas. Most will leave their upland territories after breeding and may be seen in small flocks travelling around the countryside. Some Meadow Pipits will leave this country in autumn and migrate southwards, while others arrive here from farther north.

Research has shown that Meadow Pipits which nest on higher land lay smaller clutches of eggs, but the young survive better. Cuckoos regularly search out Meadow Pipits' nests in which to lay their eggs.

Rock Pipit *Anthus spinoletta*

This pipit is to be found on rocky coasts throughout the year. Like other pipits, it has an aerial song flight, but uses rocks for take-off and landing.

Nests are built in rock crevices or on ledges, and are seldom more than 500 m from the sea. Rock Pipits feed on grassy areas near the sea or on rocky beaches where they hunt for insects and periwinkles.

In mountainous parts of Europe, another race of the Rock Pipit is found. Known as the 'Water Pipit', this race sometimes visits the British Isles in winter. It has a browner back, white outer tail feathers, a white stripe over the eye and, in spring, a pinkish breast.

Tree Pipit (1)
Sparrow-sized – 15 cm. Similar to Meadow Pipit, but slightly larger, with rather longer tail, and more stocky. May also be more yellow on breast and have more obvious, rather regular spots. Legs are pinkish. Call is hoarse 'teez'. Musical song ending with '... seea, seea, seea' as bird parachutes down to a perch.
Summer visitor to various habitats where there are trees and shrubs throughout Britain.

Meadow Pipit (2)
Sparrow-sized – 14.5 cm. Variable brown plumage with darker streaks, white outer tail feathers and, on some individuals, obvious white wing-bars. Tail is often wagged like a wagtail's. Slightly smaller than Tree Pipit, with tail a little shorter. Call is a thin 'seep'. Repetitive song given in flight.
Breeds in open country, especially upland areas. Widespread in winter.

Rock Pipit (3)
Larger than House Sparrow – 16.5 cm. Larger, darker and greyer than Meadow Pipit, with grey, not white, outer tail feathers, dark legs and longer bill. Call is 'phist', and is less squeaky than that of Meadow Pipit. Song is loud, with obvious trill at end, and is given during song flight.
Found all around British and Irish coasts except in southeast England.

Meadow
Pipits

Tree Pipit

Meadow Pipits

3 Rock Pipit
'Water Pipit'
race

Meadow Pipit

3 Rock Pipit

Tree Pipit

2 Meadow Pipit

Hilary Burn.

Yellow Wagtail *Motacilla flava*

The first Yellow Wagtails usually return to Britain from West Africa in late March or early April. From then on, they may be seen in wet meadows, where they often catch insects around the feet of grazing animals.

The species is found throughout Europe, but the plumage varies, especially the colour of the head of the male, which ranges from black to yellow. Sometimes in spring, blue-headed Yellow Wagtails from nearby western Europe are seen in Britain and have occasionally interbred with our yellow-headed Yellow Wagtails.

Although Yellow Wagtails nest on the ground, they regularly perch in trees and bushes. Their distinctive call and bounding flight help to distinguish the species when in the air.

Grey Wagtail *Motacilla cinerea*

The Grey Wagtail is seldom seen far from water. In spring and summer, it is usually to be found near fast-flowing streams and rivers in upland districts. Some pairs nest in lower areas, but nearly always near waterfalls, mill races or weirs.

Outside the breeding season, Grey Wagtails move away from the upland territories and visit slower-flowing rivers and even appear on the coast. Some – especially those from Scotland and northern England – leave the British Isles and migrate southwards into Europe. Those which remain are at risk in severe winter weather.

Pied Wagtail *Motacilla alba*

The Pied Wagtails which breed in the British Isles and nearby parts of Europe have dark grey backs and black rumps. The paler race, which is common in Europe, sometimes called the 'White Wagtail', visits Britain and Ireland on passage and sometimes breeds in Shetland.

Although Pied Wagtails are often seen near water, they are also found in dry places, running about on short grass or even flat areas such as car parks or school playgrounds. When feeding, they chase insects on or near the ground, dashing erratically, changing course suddenly and wagging their tails all the time.

In summer, they defend their breeding territories, but in winter only some males hold territories, the others flocking together. Night-time roosts may involve 1,000 or more individuals; they are often in reedbeds, but may be in bushes or trees, and some are in towns: on buildings, in greenhouses or at sewage-works. Before roosting, they gather together in open spaces.

Yellow Wagtail
Smaller than Pied Wagtail – 16.5 cm. Slim, with a long tail. Male (**1**) has bright yellow underparts, greenish black and yellow head. Female (**2**) is duller. Both sexes lose most of their yellow plumage by autumn. Juvenile (**3**) looks 'washed out' and has suggestion of black bib. Male of nearby Continental race (**4**) has bluish crown and cheeks and white stripe over eye. Call is 'tsweep'.
Summer visitor to wet meadows and marshes near the sea. Found mainly in central and southeastern England.

Grey Wagtail
Size of Pied Wagtail – 18 cm. Slim, with very long tail. Blue-grey head and back, yellow under tail, and greenish rump. Male (**5**) has black throat and yellow belly in summer. Call is shorter and more metallic than Pied Wagtail's: a sharp 'zit'.
Breeds near fast-flowing rivers, usually in upland areas. Moves to lowland areas in winter.

Pied Wagtail
18 cm. Slim, neat, black-and-white, with a long tail which is constantly wagged up and down. Female (**6**) has greyer back than male (**7**). Juvenile (**8**) is browner with dusky underparts and dark V on breast. Continental race (**9**) has pale grey back and grey rump. Flight is bounding. Call is 'chis-ick' or 'chee-wee'.
Found throughout British Isles. Usually, but not always, near water.

5 Grey Wagtail ♂

Grey Wagtail ♀

Grey Wagtail *juvenile*

8 Pied Wagtail *juvenile*

7 Pied Wagtail ♂

6 Pied Wagtail ♀

3 Yellow Wagtail *juvenile*

9 Pied Wagtail *Continental race* ♂

Yellow Wagtail *blue-headed race* ♂

1 Yellow Wagtail ♂

Yellow Wagtail ♀

Hilary Burn.

Waxwing *Bombycilla garrulus*

This exotic-looking winter visitor gets its name from curiously shaped feathers on its wings which look like pieces of red wax. It breeds in the far north of Europe and in the USSR and migrates south and west in winter. A few Waxwings reach Britain in most years and are first seen on the east coast before they move inland in their search for berries.

In some years there are invasions of Waxwings and far greater numbers are seen, which is typical of species that rely on a food supply which varies from year to year. When the population is high and food supplies become depleted, they move in huge numbers into western Europe, including Britain and, more rarely, Ireland.

Dipper *Cinclus cinclus*

Fast-flowing upland rivers and streams contain a great many invertebrates which are fed on by fish and also by the Dipper.

This species has evolved unique hunting methods: when searching for food, it wades into water and submerges, or will swim or dive. When underwater, it moves along the river bed, head into the current and wings spread to prevent it from bobbing straight up to the surface. Food is located by sight and the eye is protected by a third eye-lid which can often be seen when a Dipper is perched, as it is flicked over the eye and gives the appearance that the bird is winking.

Nests are built close to the water, often in a crevice in a rock or under a bridge. Sometimes, several Dippers will roost together under a bridge, which protects them from strong winds. The fast-flowing rivers hardly ever freeze and Dippers survive cold winters better than many other small birds.

Wren *Troglodytes troglodytes*

These birds are found in such totally different habitats as woodland, moorland, rocky islands and dense reedbeds. After a series of mild winters, when the Wren population is high, this is our most numerous breeding species. During a harsh winter, however, the number of Wrens may be reduced to only one-fifth or so, although a total recovery may take only three or four years.

Wrens sing throughout the year in order to maintain their territories. Only on winter nights do they flock together in communal roosts. Some roosts are in nest-boxes: on one occasion 63 Wrens were seen to enter one box. Another roost, in an attic, attracted 98 Wrens, all of which entered by the same small hole.

Waxwing (1)
Smaller than Starling – 18 cm. Pinkish-brown with pink crest. In flight, looks rather like Starling. Call is a trilling 'sirrr'. Often seen in flocks.
Scarce winter migrant. A few visit eastern Britain most years with many more during 'invasions'.

Dipper (2)
Smaller than Starling – 18 cm. Dumpy, with short tail. Adult appears black with chestnut belly and white 'bib'. Juveniles are greyer. Flight is fast, direct and often close to the water. Perches on rocks where it 'bobs'. Call is a short 'zit'. Song is a sweet warbling.
Found near fast-flowing water, mainly in upland areas. Visits lower rivers in winter, when it may even be seen on the coast.

Wren (3)
Tiny – 9.5 cm. Dumpy, with short tail which is often cocked up. Dark brown with paler underparts and pale stripe over eye. Call is a hard 'tic-tic' or forceful trill. Song is a loud, fast warbling, usually with a trill near the end, the tiny bird appearing to tremble with emotion.
Found throughout the British Isles; especially common where there is dense vegetation.

Starlings

Waxwings

1 Waxwings

3 Wrens

2 Dipper

Hilary Burn

Dunnock *Prunella modularis*

The familiar Dunnock is frequently overlooked by non-birdwatchers, yet it is found commonly in parks and gardens as well as in woodland and even on moorland or rocky islands. On farmland, it is one of the most numerous breeding birds.

Despite one of their old names – 'Hedge Sparrow' – Dunnocks are not related to sparrows: they have the thin bill typical of species which feed mainly on insects. One old country name for the Dunnock was 'Shuffle-wing' which referred to its habit of flicking open one wing above its back in a kind of display. As with most song birds, territories are established during the breeding season, though in many cases Dunnock territories are occupied not only by a male and a female, but also by one or more other adults which may help to feed the young. Winter territories are also established and sometimes occupied by small groups of Dunnocks.

Robin *Erithacus rubecula*

This is Britain's national bird. It is common in parks and gardens and often becomes tame; elsewhere in Europe, however, it is rather shy and difficult to observe. It defends a territory in both summer and winter and may be heard singing in most months of the year. After the breeding season, until about January, the Robin's song is different – slower and rather sad. Males and females occupy separate territories in winter. While males seldom move far from their breeding areas, the females may move farther afield, and some even leave the country.

Robins have elaborate displays in which their red breast plays an important part as a visual danger signal to other Robins which enter an occupied territory.

Robins usually nest in a hollow on a bank or in a hedge, but they will also nest in odd places such as garden sheds or in old tin cans which are lodged in hedges. They feed mainly on insects, although they also eat berries and worms. Although, on average, Robins live only a little more than a year, some adults have long lives, and at least one survived 11 years.

Bluethroat *Luscinia svecica*

These birds breed in continental Europe and winter in Africa. A few occur here on migration; most arrive in autumn and belong to the red-spotted race in which the male in spring has a red spot in the centre of his blue throat; Bluethroats of the white-spotted race from central Europe are seen less often. They are usually very secretive and difficult to observe.

Dunnock (1)
Sparrow-sized – 14.5 cm. Rather secretive. Brown streaky plumage with grey head and breast. The bill is thin. Feeds with body held close to the ground and moves with mouse-like jerks. Frequently flicks its wings. Call is a loud piping 'tseep' and song is a Wren-like warble, but slower, less forceful and with no trills.
Widespread throughout British Isles. Usually found near trees or bushes.

Robin (2)
Sparrow-sized – 14 cm. Upright, and often appearing plump, with red face and breast and white belly. Male and female look alike. Juvenile (3) lacks any red and is speckled. Call is a loud 'tic, tic'. Attractive warbling song is heard in spring, but it also has a different, slower, sadder song in autumn and winter.
Common throughout the British Isles, except in far north. Usually found near trees or bushes.

Bluethroat
Size of Robin – 14 cm. Slim with white stripe over eye and reddish patches at base of dark brown tail. In spring, the male (4) has a brilliant blue throat with, depending upon its race, either a red spot or a white spot in the centre. Females have a pale throat. In autumn, juveniles (5) have a variety of different throat patterns. Call is a sharp 'tacc, tacc'.
Seen mainly on the British east coast in autumn.

1 Dunnock

3 Robin
juvenile

2 Robins

5 Bluethroat
juvenile

Dunnock

4 Bluethroat
red-spotted race ♂

Hilary Burn

Nightingale *Luscinia megarhynchos*

These birds may sing at any time of day or night, but it is after dusk or before dawn, when most other birds are silent, that their magnificent song can best be heard. On a calm night, it can carry for up to a mile. In Britain, Nightingales are highly secretive and spend much of their time in dense bushes or on the ground where they hunt for worms, spiders and insects. They generally sing from dense cover, although elsewhere in Europe they are often rather easier to see.

Nightingales winter in central Africa and usually return to Britain in mid April. Males return first and their song may be heard until late May or early June when the young hatch. The favourite habitat is deciduous woodland with dense ground cover.

In some parts of Britain Nightingales have declined during this century, but in southeast England, where numbers are largest, the population seems to be stable in spite of great fluctuations from year to year.

Black Redstart *Phoenicurus ochruros*

The Second World War left many ugly bomb-sites and derelict buildings in London which were quickly colonised by the Black Redstart which had, until then, been a very rare breeding species. The number of Black Redstarts breeding in Britain is still not large, but has continued to grow slowly. Buildings in central and southeastern Britain continue to be used, but some nests are built in natural holes in cliffs.

Adult male Black Redstarts are unmistakable, but some start to breed before they have fully adult plumage. Black Redstarts are seen at all seasons of the year, but especially in spring and autumn when some on passage from continental Europe are also seen.

Redstart *Phoenicurus phoenicurus*

In parts of Europe the Redstart is very common around towns and villages and will occupy sites similar to those used by the Black Redstart. In Britain, however, Redstarts nest mainly in holes in trees or walls and even on the ground.

Redstarts feed mainly on insects. The male catches much of his prey in flight while the female feeds more often on the ground. The red tail, which gives the species its name, is used in display.

The species has become rarer since 1969 when a number of British breeding birds which winter in Africa were affected by prolonged drought in the Sahel region, on the southern fringe of the Sahara.

Nightingale (1)
Rather like a large Robin – 16.5 cm. Rich brown upperparts, reddish tail and large eyes. Very secretive. Juveniles are spotted. Loud, rich song is repetitive with long pauses and may be heard by day as well as by night. *Summer visitor to woods and dense thickets in southeastern England.*

Black Redstart
Size of Robin – 14 cm. Robin-like and rather active. Often perches on ground or on rocks or walls. Adult male (**2**) has dark grey body, pale patch on wings and rusty red tail. Female (**3**) and juvenile have paler bodies and lack pale patch on wings. Alarm call is a hard 'tucc, tucc'. Song is fast warble followed by a rattle. *Present throughout the year. Breeds in ruined buildings, power-stations, and also on sea cliffs. Usually seen near the coast in winter.*

Redstart
Size of Robin – 14 cm. Very active, regularly quivering its rusty red tail. Male (**4**) has reddish underparts, grey crown and white forehead. Female (**5**) and juvenile have greyish-brown backs and buff underparts. Call is 'hooveet'; has warbling song with a strange jangle. *Summer visitor. Nests in holes in trees or walls. Found in woods, parks, heaths and moors mainly in northern and western Britain.*

4 Redstart ♂

5 Redstart ♀

2 Black Redstart ♂

3 Black Redstart ♀

1 Nightingales

Hilary Burn

Whinchat *Saxicola rubetra*

The Whinchat and Stonechat are closely related, yet Stonechats are mainly resident in the British Isles whereas the Whinchats are summer migrants which winter in tropical Africa. Whinchats will feed on spiders or worms, but most of their food is insects, many of which are caught as they visit flowers.

Whinchats have declined in numbers this century, especially in southeast England, and are now most common in upland areas. Recently, however, there have been signs of a slight recovery, perhaps because many pairs have taken to breeding in young conifer plantations.

Stonechat *Saxicola torquata*

The Stonechat gets its name from its sharp call which sounds like two pebbles being knocked together.

Those Stonechats which remain in their breeding territories during the winter are at risk, and a great many die during icy weather. Numbers can, however, recover quickly after a severe winter, as Stonechats are capable of rearing three broods in a summer, which may produce 15 juveniles; although it has been shown that, on average, half of those juveniles will die during their first three weeks out of the nest.

Like most species, Stonechats moult their feathers after breeding. The male's new head feathers are black, but they have buff tips which give a dull mottled appearance. During the winter the buff tips wear away, leaving a smart black head by the next breeding season.

Wheatear *Oenanthe oenanthe*

This is often the first migrant to be seen in the British Isles in spring. In some years, the first Wheatears appear before the end of February, but most arrive in late March or early April, with a second rush in May. These later Wheatears often belong to the brighter and larger Greenland race which stop off en route for their breeding grounds.

Wheatears make amazing migratory journeys. They all winter in Africa, south of the Sahara, and as well as some migrating northwest to Greenland, others migrate northeast across Asia to nest in Alaska. Those from Greenland fly direct to Spain on their autumn migration: a non-stop journey of 3,200 km across the Atlantic.

Wheatears nest in burrows, among stones or in stone walls. Their song is attractive and often given during a fluttering song flight. They also sometimes hover like tiny Kestrels when on the lookout for food or predators.

Whinchat
Smaller than Robin – 12.5 cm. Short-tailed. Often perches upright on fences or low bushes. Male (**1**) has white stripe over eye, white patches on wings and at base of tail. Female (**2**) is similar, but paler. Juvenile has a faint stripe over eye. Call is a sharp 'tic, tic'.
Summer visitor to open areas with some bushes, especially in north and west of Britain and parts of Ireland. Seen elsewhere on migration.

Stonechat
Smaller than Robin – 12.5 cm. Short-tailed and plump. Often perches on tops of bushes or on wires. Male in summer (**3**) has black head, white on neck and orangish breast. Female (**4**) and juvenile are less colourful. Call is sharp 'tac, tac'. Usually seen in open areas with some bushes, especially gorse. *Most common in heathland and especially coastal localities (where it is relatively mild in winter).*

Wheatear
Larger than Robin – 15 cm. White rump and short black tail. Often perches on the ground where it stands very upright. Male in spring (**5**) has black cheeks, blue-grey back and sandy breast. Female (**6**), juvenile (**7**) and male in autumn look paler and 'washed out'. Call is a hard 'chack, chack'.
Summer visitor to uplands and some coastal localities. Seen elsewhere on migration.

Whinchat

Wheatear   Stonechat

Wheatear
Greenland race ♂

Whinchats 1 ♂

2 ♀

7 *juvenile*

6 ♀

Wheatears

5 ♂   3 ♂

winter ♂

4 ♀

Hilary Burn

Stonechats

Ring Ouzel *Turdus torquatus*

This is the blackbird of mountain areas. It breeds in wild, hilly country where there are crags and rocky gullies. Its loud, sweet, simple song is repeated from a prominent perch, and echoes amongst the rocks. In autumn, it flies south to winter in southern Europe or North Africa.

Ring Ouzels have declined during this century while Blackbirds have become more numerous and spread northwards. It is possible that because the two species are closely related there is some competition between them, and Blackbirds have taken over some of the territories once occupied by Ring Ouzels.

Blackbird *Turdus merula*

This familiar bird is recognizable, even at a distance, by the way it moves and especially by the way it raises its tail on landing. These small details which help to identify a species are called by birdwatchers its 'jizz'.

Originally, Blackbirds probably lived on the edge of woodland, but they have adapted to living on farmland as well as in parks and gardens. Now, Blackbirds which nest on farms and in gardens are more successful at producing young than those in woodland. Juveniles in towns, however, are commonly caught by domestic cats.

A Blackbird may often be seen (or heard) turning over dead leaves under trees or bushes as it searches for worms, insects, millipedes or small snails. Many kinds of fruit, especially berries, are also eaten. Like many other species, it does not digest the hard parts of its food, but ejects them through its beak in the form of pellets.

In some parts of northern Britain, Blackbirds leave their breeding grounds for the winter, but elsewhere they are resident and may be joined by others from Europe. They seem to be able to survive cold weather quite well: after the very cold winter of 1962–3, the Blackbird population fell by 18% whereas that of the Song Thrush fell by 57%.

During a mild spell in winter, Blackbirds may start to nest, but young hatched at that time seldom survive. By April, the first clutch of eggs has usually been laid and this will be followed by two, or occasionally three more.

Ring Ouzel
Slightly smaller than Blackbird – 24 cm. Male (**1**) is sooty black with white crescent on breast and pale patch on wing. Female (**2**) is scaly brown with pale crescent on breast. Juvenile often lacks mark on breast, but is greyer than a juvenile Blackbird. Song is clear piping; call is loud, hard 'tac, tac'.
Summer visitor to mountains and moorland. Sometimes near coasts in spring and autumn.

Blackbird
25 cm. Male (**3**) is all black with yellow bill and eye-ring. Female (**4**) is dark brown, often with pale chin and rather spotted brown breast. Juvenile (**5**) is reddish-brown with speckled brown breast. Immature male (**6**) has dark bill and browner plumage than adult. Has chinking alarm call or scolding 'tuc, tuc'. Song is clear and fluty, but tails off at end.
Found throughout the British Isles, except in very mountainous country.

Ring Ouzel ♂

6 Blackbird *immature* ♂

2 Ring Ouzel ♀

1 Ring Ouzel ♂

4 Blackbird ♀

5 Blackbird *juvenile*

3 Blackbird ♂

Hilary Burn.

Song Thrush *Turdus philomelos*

On a warm summer evening, it is the Song Thrush's song which resounds through much of our countryside and is often the last song to be heard before the woods become dark and the only sounds are those of truly nocturnal creatures. The song is simple, but attractive: a short phrase is repeated several times, then apparently discarded in favour of another which is, in turn, repeated and discarded and so on until the first phrase returns again.

Song Thrushes feed on worms, insects, fruits and, of course, snails. Snails are usually eaten in summer when they are plentiful and when other food is sometimes scarce. A Song Thrush which finds a snail takes it to a hard object, which is usually a stone, but may be a dead branch, a tin can or a bottle, and then hits it against this 'anvil' until the shell breaks; the snail is then wiped on the ground several times before being eaten.

In autumn, Song Thrushes turn to berries, especially yew berries, as a source of food. Our native birds are then joined by migrant Song Thrushes from northern or eastern Europe which share the harvest of berries until they eventually run out and worms become an important food again.

Redwing *Turdus iliacus*

Listen carefully on a calm autumn night and you may hear the thin 'tseep' of migrating Redwings. Redwings migrate by day and by night, but it is after dark that their flight-calls are especially valuable in helping to keep flocks together. Morning will often find parties of newly arrived Redwings stripping the berries from our hedges, usually in the company of Song Thrushes, Fieldfares and Blackbirds. In the evenings, Redwings gather together in large communal roosts.

Flocks of Redwings move around the British Isles in winter, especially in very cold weather. Then they may be seen in town gardens, on playing fields or on other areas of short grass. During prolonged frosts, many fail to find sufficient food and die.

Two races of Redwings visit the British Isles in winter: many cross the North Sea from Scandinavia while another, slightly larger, race migrates here from Iceland. Redwings have started to colonise the British Isles: the first pair was found in Scotland in 1925, then large numbers were discovered in the 1950s and 1960s; despite a recent decrease a few pairs still nest each year.

Song Thrush (1)
Smaller than Blackbird – 23 cm. Brown above, pale below with many small spots on breast. Orange underwing shows in flight. Call is a sharp 'sipp'. Song is loud and sweetly repetitive. Juvenile has buff streaks on back. *Breeds almost anywhere if there are trees or bushes.*

Redwing (2)
Smaller than Blackbird – 21 cm. Like rather dark Song Thrush with white stripe over eye, reddish flanks and dark red (not orange) under the wing. Flight call is a high-pitched 'tseep'. *Mainly a winter visitor. A few pairs nest in Scotland.*

Redwing

Song Thrush

Redwings

Fieldfare

Song Thrush

Blackbird ♀

Mistle Thrush

2 Redwing

1 Song Thrush

Hilary Burn

Fieldfare *Turdus pilaris*

As winter approaches, flocks of thrushes leave Scandinavia, cross the North Sea, and arrive in the British Isles. Fieldfares are one of these migrants, and their noisy, rather ragged-looking flocks can be seen moving around farmland between October and April. On winter evenings they often gather in large, communal roosts and spend the night in dense bushes.

These migrants from the north join other, resident thrushes and take advantage of the supply of berries and other fruits which are usually found in plenty in our countryside in autumn. Fieldfares also find food in orchards where they feed on windfalls. Later in winter, when the fruits have gone, they turn to worms and any insect food they can find.

During the last hundred years the Fieldfare has been spreading to new areas in Europe, and recently it has colonised Iceland and Greenland. In 1967, it nested in Britain for the first time and a few pairs have nested regularly since then. In Scandinavia, colonies of Fieldfares nest in town parks and gardens as well as in birch woods and other habitats; it remains to be seen whether they will, in time, colonise towns in the British Isles.

Mistle Thrush *Turdus viscivorus*

As storm clouds gather and the wind strengthens, many species stop singing and take cover. Not the Mistle Thrush: in these conditions, it can often be heard singing strongly, while perched at the top of a tall tree. Not surprisingly, this habit has earned the Mistle Thrush the old country name of 'Stormcock'.

In autumn, Mistle Thrushes travel around the countryside in noisy, chattering flocks as they gradually strip the ripe berries from the trees and bushes. In many areas, they start with the rowan, or mountain ash, and may often be seen on remote moorland in search of this food supply. In towns and villages, they may gorge themselves on berries from churchyard yew trees or hunt for worms in parks and gardens or on playing fields.

Mistle Thrushes have not always been so widespread. Until about 1800, they were found only in southern England or Wales, but then they spread into Ireland and northwards in Britain until, now, they are common everywhere but the far north of Scotland.

Fieldfare (1)
Slightly larger than Blackbird – 25.5 cm. Chestnut back, dark tail, grey head and grey rump. Call is a noisy, laughing chuckle: 'chack-chack, chack'. Usually seen in flocks. Flight often appears lazy, and white underwing is obvious.
Winter visitor to the British Isles. A few remain in summer and nest.

Mistle Thrush (2)
Larger than Blackbird – 27 cm. Larger, greyer and more upright than Song Thrush, and also appears to have a smaller head. Outer tail feathers show white in flight. Breast is pale, with large spots. Flight looks leisurely, with wings closing at regular intervals. Underwing is white. Juvenile (3) has pale, spotted head and streaky back. Call is a chattering rattle. Song is loud, clear and rather like that of Blackbird.
Found throughout the British Isles, except in the far north.

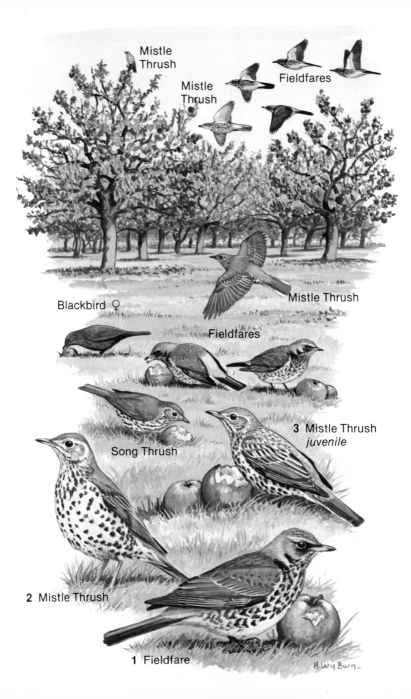

Mistle
Thrush

Mistle
Thrush

Fieldfares

Mistle Thrush

Blackbird ♀

Fieldfares

Song Thrush

3 Mistle Thrush
juvenile

2 Mistle Thrush

1 Fieldfare

Hilary Burn

Cetti's Warbler *Cettia cetti*

The arrival of the Cetti's Warbler in Britain and its colonisation are quite remarkable. At the beginning of this century, it was found mainly around the Mediterranean, but more northerly areas were gradually colonized and in 1972 it was found nesting in Britain for the first time. Since then, its colonisation of Britain has continued.

Unlike most of our warblers, Cetti's does not migrate for the winter: yet it does feed on insects, which means that prolonged periods of cold weather are likely to affect the population. So far, however, Cetti's appears to be able to withstand our cold weather rather better than do many other small birds which also feed on insects.

A male Cetti's Warbler may have two or more females, but he takes no part in nest-building or incubating the eggs, and helps only a little with rearing the young. Song is heard mostly during the day but unpaired males may sing after dark.

Grasshopper Warbler *Locustella naevia*

The amazing, reeling song of this secretive warbler is usually the only clue to its presence. Since human hearing deteriorates with age, this bird's high-pitched trill, which may continue for a minute or more without a break, becomes increasingly hard to hear as one becomes older.

Grasshopper Warblers usually sing from dense cover, and move through vegetation rather like mice. They have surprisingly long middle toes, which apparently help them to grip several stems at once and give them extra support when moving around in dense undergrowth. Much of their time is spent on or near the ground.

Although their amazing song may frequently be heard in daylight, dawn and dusk are probably the best times to hear it. Song may also be heard after dark, and some individuals will sing all through the night.

Savi's Warbler *Locustella luscinioides*

Although closely related to the Grasshopper Warbler, the Savi's Warbler looks rather like a Reed Warbler and lives in dense reedbeds with scattered bushes, which it may use as song-posts.

In the past, Savi's Warblers regularly nested in the Fens of East Anglia, but became extinct by 1856. They are now nesting here again, and are, at present, continuing to increase and colonise new reedbeds.

Cetti's Warbler (1)
Size of Great Tit – 14 cm. Secretive. Rather dumpy, like large Wren. Reddish-brown back, paler underparts and pale stripe over eye. Tail is very rounded and often cocked up. Call is a short 'twick' or loud 'chee'. Song starts suddenly and is fast and loud.
Resident in wet, densely vegetated places in southern and eastern England.

Grasshopper Warbler (2)
Smaller than Great Tit – 13 cm. Rather secretive. Brown, streaked upperparts, paler underparts and rounded tail. Song is a long, high-pitched, drawn-out, insect-like trill, often heard at dusk or even after dark.
A summer visitor to most parts of the British Isles where there is thick, low vegetation. Often found in damp places or in young plantations.

Savi's Warbler (3)
Size of Great Tit – 14 cm. Rather like large Reed Warbler. Buff-coloured plumage, paler breast and whitish chin. Tail is rounded. Call is a sharp 'spitz'. Song is a buzz, rather like Grasshopper Warbler's trill, but faster and lower-pitched.
Summer visitor to a few large reedbeds, mainly in southern England.

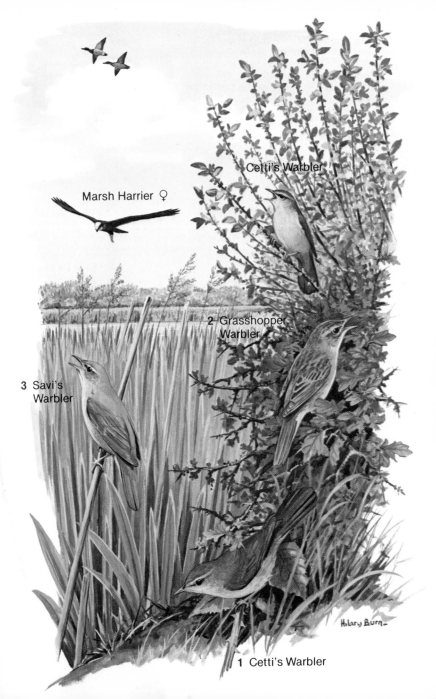

Cetti's Warbler

Marsh Harrier ♀

2 Grasshopper Warbler

3 Savi's Warbler

Hilary Burn

1 Cetti's Warbler

Sedge Warbler *Acrocephalus schoenobaenus*

Dense waterside vegetation is the normal breeding site for the Sedge Warbler. In some places, it even nests in reedbeds, close to Reed Warblers, but in other places it chooses drier sites, such as damp ditches and even young conifer plantations.

Sedge Warblers arrive in April or early May; they rear one or two broods before feeding up in readiness for their return flight to Africa. Most Sedge Warblers make the journey across Europe, the Mediterranean and the Sahara Desert in one single flight. To make this amazing journey, they store body-fat from which they get the necessary energy. Many birds store fat and increase their weight by about 30%, but the Sedge Warbler almost doubles its weight just before it migrates.

The Sedge Warbler population appears to have fallen in recent years, perhaps because of the drought in the Sahel region south of the Sahara, which means they now have even farther to fly without a break.

Marsh Warbler *Acrocephalus palustris*

Widespread over much of Europe and closely related to both Reed and Sedge Warblers, Marsh Warblers nest in only a very few places in southern Britain.

Marsh Warblers are superb mimics, and have been heard to copy the songs or calls of over 50 other species.

Reed Warbler *Acrocephalus scirpaceus*

These birds prefer to nest in dense, wet reedbeds, where they generally breed in colonies, but they will sometimes nest in drier areas. Reedbeds give the nests protection from ground predators, but they are more likely to be raided from the air, especially by Cuckoos, which regularly lay their eggs in Reed Warblers' nests.

Rough weather also causes problems for Reed Warblers, as many nests will be beaten to the ground, and in wet or cold summers adults will have difficulty in finding enough food for their young. To overcome these seasonal food shortages, Reed Warblers incubate their eggs before the clutch is complete, which results in the eggs hatching at different times. In poor seasons, only the eldest will survive, while in good years all will live. This arrangement, known as asynchronous hatching, is common among birds of prey.

Many colonies of Reed Warblers have disappeared as a result of drainage and river management, which have reduced the number of natural reedbeds. The birds have, however, benefited from many new reedbeds in flooded sand- or gravel-pits.

Sedge Warbler (1)
Smaller than Great Tit – 13 cm. Streaked back, orange-brown rump and flanks, white stripe over eye and dark crown. Call is a loud 'tuc'. Warbling song has grating trills and sparrow-like chirrups. Sings from a perch, or in a short display flight. *Summer visitor to most lowland parts of Britain and Ireland and is usually found near water.*

Marsh Warbler (2)
Size of Reed Warbler – 12.5 cm. Very similar to Reed Warbler, but plumage appears less rufous, throat is paler and bill is a little stouter. Best distinction is song: musical and varied, with imitation of many songs and calls. Often sings from an exposed perch. *Small numbers of these summer visitors breed in Britain. Likes nettle beds or dense willows near water.*

Reed Warbler (3)
Smaller than Great Tit – 12.5 cm. Plain brown back, rich brown rump and pale underparts. Bill is long, and forehead steep. Hard churring call and long, fast, churring, repetitive, warbling song. *Summer visitor to dense reedbeds in England and Wales.*

Aquatic Warbler (4)
Size of Sedge Warbler – 12.5 cm. Rather rare and secretive. Yellow streak on crown, bold black stripes on back, and streaked rump. *Passage migrant seen in reedbeds mainly in autumn.*

1 Sedge Warbler

4 Aquatic Warbler

Sedge Warbler *juvenile*

3 Reed Warbler

2 Marsh Warbler

Cuckoo *juvenile*

Hilary Burn

Dartford Warbler *Sylvia undata*

The Dartford Warbler takes its English name from Dartford Heath in Kent, where the species was first identified. It no longer breeds at Dartford, and its population has declined. Lowland heaths with large expanses of gorse are its favourite habitat, but these have, for too long, been regarded as 'wasteland' and most have either been ploughed up or had houses built on them. The heaths of Hampshire and Dorset are the last stronghold for this species.

Dartfords do not migrate and, being mainly insect-eaters, suffer in severe winters when their food is hard to find. After a series of mild winters, numbers often build up again and other heaths in southern England are colonised.

Lesser Whitethroat *Sylvia curruca*

In many parts of England and Wales, this warbler is much more common than is generally realised, but unless one is familiar with its song the Lesser Whitethroat is easily overlooked. In addition, its song is usually heard for only a few weeks after its return in spring. Adults can, however, be noisy when their young have just fledged, in late summer.

The Lesser Whitethroats which breed in Britain probably winter in Ethiopia or the Sudan, in northeast Africa. Most of those which leave Britain in autumn fly to north Italy and from there fly southwards across the Mediterranean and straight to their winter quarters. In spring, they return by a different route, around the eastern end of the Mediterranean and then straight to Britain.

Whitethroat *Sylvia communis*

Until 1969, the Whitethroat was one of our most numerous summer visitors, but in that year observers all over western Europe noticed that only small numbers had returned and, later, research showed that the population had fallen by 77% in one year, thus presenting one of the most curious ornithological mysteries ever recorded.

Scientists have now deduced that the disappearance of the Whitethroat was caused by severe drought in the Sahel zone of Africa, the area in which western European Whitethroats wintered. Many must have died because of the sudden climatic change. Although numbers of Whitethroats have increased again, they are still well below the level of 1968.

Dartford Warbler
Smaller than Great Tit – 12.5 cm. Small and dark, with a long tail. Male (1) has dark brown upperparts, grey head and reddish underparts. Female (2) and juvenile are paler. Usually very secretive, but will sing from the top of bushes. Call is a grating 'tchirr'.
Resident on a few heaths in southern England.

Lesser Whitethroat (3)
Smaller than Great Tit – 13.5 cm. Small, grey and secretive. Has white throat and dark cheeks. Back is greyer than that of Whitethroat, and lacks any reddish-brown in wing. Call is a sharp 'tacc'. The song starts with a quiet warble followed by a loud rattle of one note repeated several times, rather like the start of the song of Yellowhammer.
Summer visitor to places with thick cover or thick hedges, mainly in southern and eastern England and parts of Wales. Rare in Scotland and does not breed in Ireland.

Whitethroat
Size of Great Tit – 14 cm. Male (4) has grey head, white throat and reddish-brown wings. Female (5) and juvenile have brown heads. Call is a hard 'chack' or scolding 'tchurr'. Song is an unmusical jumble of phrases, often given during a short song flight (6).
Summer visitor to patches of scrub in most parts of lowland Britain and Ireland.

6 Whitethroat *display*

4 Whitethroat ♂

1 Dartford Warbler ♂

5 Whitethroat ♀

2 Dartford Warbler ♀

3 Lesser Whitethroat

Hilary Burn

Icterine Warbler *Hippolais icterina*

This species is widespread over much of central and eastern Europe, but is a rather rare visitor to Britain. In autumn, juvenile Willow Warblers with bright yellow breasts are sometimes mistaken for Icterine Warblers.

Melodious Warbler *Hippolais polyglotta*

The Melodious Warbler is most common in southwest Europe and usually visits Britain only in autumn. Most occur in southwest Britain and Ireland, mirroring the European breeding distribution.

Barred Warbler *Sylvia nisoria*

This regular autumn visitor from central and eastern Europe is more numerous in some years than in others. It spends much of the time moving clumsily around in dense cover, such as elder bushes and clumps of ivy, where it feeds on berries as well as insects. Almost all the Barred Warblers seen in Britain are juveniles.

Garden Warbler *Sylvia borin*

Despite its name, this warbler is not common in gardens. Like other warblers, the Garden Warbler is rather secretive and best located by its song. Although most warblers can be easily identified by their songs, the similarity between those of Blackcap and Garden Warbler is so great that even experienced ornithologists often need to see the bird to confirm its identity.

Garden Warblers are rare in northern Scotland and Ireland. They arrive in April or May after wintering in central or southern Africa.

Blackcap *Sylvia atricapilla*

In the opinion of some people, the song of the Blackcap is as good as, if not better than, that of any other British bird. In spring and early summer, its song can be heard in woodland with thick undergrowth, especially thick bramble bushes.

Until recently, Blackcaps were considered to be summer migrants which left in autumn for southern Europe or North Africa. Now, however, they are seen regularly in midwinter, particularly in western and southwestern England and in Ireland, where they often visit gardens. These wintering Blackcaps are from northern Europe and appear to have learned to supplement their natural diet of insects and berries with food from birdtables, where they are sometimes aggressive towards other garden birds.

Icterine Warbler (1)
Larger than Willow Warbler – 13.5 cm. Yellow-and-green, with bluish legs, long bill with wide base, peaked crown, pale eye-ring, long wings with, usually, a pale panel. Underparts paler, with almost no yellow in autumn.
Seen mainly on British east coast in autumn.

Melodious Warbler (2)
Larger than Willow Warbler – 13 cm. Wide based, long bill. Often has flatter head, browner paler legs, browner back and shorter wings than Icterine.
Rare visitor mainly to coastal areas in autumn.

Barred Warbler
Larger than Great Tit – 15 cm. Large, clumsy greyish warbler with domed head and heavy bill. 1st-winter (3) is brown, with little barring, has dark eye and pale edges to wing feathers. Call is a sharp 'tchack' or 'tcharr'.
Mainly seen in autumn on British east coast.

Garden Warbler (4)
Size of Great Tit – 14 cm. Plain brown back with paler underparts and no obvious marks. Call is sharp 'check'. Song is a fast, even, musical warble.
Summer visitor to woods, scrub or young plantations.

Blackcap
Size of Great Tit – 14 cm. Rather grey. Male (5) has black cap. Female (6) and juvenile have brown caps. Call is hard 'tacc'. Shorter, richer and more varied song than Garden Warbler.
Mainly summer visitor. Scarce in north and west.

2 Melodious Warbler

1 Icterine Warbler

4 Garden Warbler

6 Blackcap ♀

3 Barred Warbler *1st-winter*

5 Blackcap ♂

Hilary Burn

Chiffchaff *Phylloscopus collybita*

Willow Warblers and Chiffchaffs look so similar that, unless they are heard singing, it is usually difficult to identify them with certainty – such birds are sometimes referred to as Willow/Chiffs.

Although a few Chiffchaffs are seen in southern Britain in winter, most winter in France or around the western Mediterranean and return in late March or early April. Their song, often heard from leafless branches of a tree, is usually the first clue that spring migration is underway.

This species is always restless, flicking its wings and tail, or flitting from one branch to another. Like other warblers, it will sometimes catch insects on the wing like a flycatcher. Sometimes, Chiffchaffs and Willow Warblers will hover and pick insects from under leaves.

Willow Warbler *Phylloscopus trochilus*

The Willow Warbler, our most numerous summer visitor, arrives in April and returns, in early autumn, to its winter quarters in central and southern Africa.

Individuals differ in the amount of yellow in the plumage: some may appear brown-and-white, while others, especially young in autumn, may be very yellow.

Like other warblers, it feeds chiefly on insects and spiders.

The mortality rate of all birds is highest in their first year and the Willow Warbler is no exception. Perhaps only one-quarter of those hatched in one year will be alive the following spring. There is, however, a record of one Willow Warbler surviving into its sixth year in spite of its long migration.

Wood Warbler *Phylloscopus sibilatrix*

A particularly attractive warbler which arrives in Britain in late April and leaves again in September. It spends the winter in central Africa.

Its song can be heard in mature woods with little ground cover. When singing from a perch, its whole body shakes, but sometimes the song is given as it flies from branch to branch. The male has a butterfly-like display and will spiral down to the woodland floor.

In southeastern England, the Wood Warbler has been becoming scarcer in recent years, but in Scotland it may still be spreading northwards.

Chiffchaff (1)
Smaller than Blue Tit – 11 cm. Best identified by song 'zip-zap, zap, zip-zap . . .'. Brown above, pale below, pale stripe over eye, some individuals slightly more yellow. Legs usually dark. *Mainly a summer visitor to woods with thick undergrowth and places with mixed bushes and trees. Rather scarce in northern Scotland and in upland areas.*

Willow Warbler (2)
Smaller than Blue Tit – 11 cm. Difficult to tell from Chiffchaff, but song is series of notes trickling down the scale. Some are more yellow than others. Legs and feet are pale. Juvenile in autumn (3) is more yellow than adult. *Summer visitor to most parts of Britain and Ireland. Found in woods, scrub and almost treeless areas.*

Wood Warbler
Slightly larger than Willow Warbler – 13 cm. Adult (4) has yellow-green back, bright yellow throat and breast, sharply divided from pure white belly, and yellow stripe over eye. Juvenile (5) is duller. Song is either a repetitive 'duu' or a single note repeated faster and faster and ending in a trill. *Summer visitor to mature woodland, especially oak and beech. Scarce in southeast England and northern Scotland. Rare in Ireland.*

4 Wood
Warbler

5 Wood Warbler
juvenile

1 Chiffchaff

Chiffchaff
juvenile

3 Willow Warbler
juvenile

Hilary Burn

2 Willow Warbler

Goldcrest *Regulus regulus*

These birds can be surprisingly difficult to see although they are relatively common. The best method of locating one is to sit quietly in a conifer wood and listen for its thin call or high-pitched song. In autumn and winter, they will rove through all types of woodland and often join small flocks of tits. Once located, a Goldcrest may appear quite tame and come close.

While searching for their insect food, they frequently hang upside down or hover to pick insects from the undersides of leaves. Their beautiful nests are made from moss, woven together with spiders' webs, and often hang under dense foliage towards the end of a branch.

Goldcrests and Firecrests appear the same size, but Goldcrests generally have fractionally shorter tails and may be a little lighter, which makes them the smallest bird found wild in the British Isles. It is amazing to think of such a tiny bird making migratory flights across the open sea, but many do exactly that. Although most of our Goldcrests are resident, many in Europe are migrants and each autumn a lot cross the North Sea from northern Europe to winter in Britain.

Like many other small birds, Goldcrests suffer in cold winter weather, and after a particularly severe spell the population falls dramatically. In general, however, numbers appear to be increasing, and the species must have been helped by the many conifer plantations which have recently been established.

Firecrest *Regulus ignicapillus*

For many years, Firecrests were usually seen only in spring and autumn as they reached the British Isles while on migration, although a few were also seen in winter. On the Continent, Firecrests have been colonising new areas, and in 1962 this species was discovered breeding in southern England.

The number of pairs which nest here is still small and varies greatly from year to year, but it seems as if the Firecrest will colonise parts of Britain, especially places where there are mature conifers within mixed woodland plantations with open spaces.

Like Goldcrests, Firecrests are very active and often secretive; their songs or calls make it less difficult for the birdwatcher to locate them.

In late autumn, the very rare Yellow-browed Warbler *Phylloscopus inornatus* from Siberia may be seen on the coast. It recalls an uncrested Goldcrest with a stripe over its eye or a small Willow Warbler with one large and one small wing-bar on each wing.

Goldcrest
Smaller than Wren – 9 cm. Tiny and very active. Greenish, rather dumpy with short tail. Eye is noticeably large at close range. Orange-and-black crown of male (**1**) and yellow-and-orange crown of female (**2**) can be difficult to observe. Juvenile (**3**) lacks the yellow crown. Call is high-pitched 'zit'. Song is two high notes repeated rapidly, finishing with a short trill.
Resident in conifer woods in all parts of the British Isles, but also regularly visits deciduous woods.

Firecrest (4)
Size of Goldcrest – 9 cm. Similar to Goldcrest, but with dark line through eye and broad white stripe over eye. More contrast between greener back (often bronze tint on sides of nape) and whiter underparts. 'Zit, zit', call is lower in pitch than that of Goldcrest and the harsher song has no trill.
Rare breeding species mainly in southern England, but occurs on passage on south and east coasts in spring and autumn.

4 Firecrest

Firecrest
juvenile

Goldcrests

2 ♀

3 *juvenile*

1 Goldcrest

♂

Coal Tit

Yellow-browed Warbler

Hilary Burn

Spotted Flycatcher *Muscicapa striata*

This is one of the last summer visitors to arrive, as the largest numbers do not reach the British Isles until the second or third week of May. One or rarely two broods of young are reared before the Spotted Flycatcher leaves again between July and October.

A Spotted Flycatcher feeds almost entirely on insects, which it generally catches in the air by fluttering out from a perch, twisting and turning, then seizing its prey and returning to the same or a nearby perch. It is often this hunting flight which first attracts one's attention to this small brown bird. Many other small birds will also fly up and catch insects in the air, but none do so as regularly as the flycatchers.

The most usual habitat for Spotted Flycatchers is the edge of woodland or glades in woods, but they will also visit gardens, especially large ones with mature trees. Their neat nest is often situated amongst vegetation against the trunk of a tree or a wall. They will, however, build in old nests of other species and, like Robins, sometimes use open-fronted nest-boxes or even old tin cans.

Red-breasted Flycatcher *Ficedula parva*

In autumn, many small passage migrants which should be moving south through Europe get off course and arrive tired on the east coast of Britain. Juveniles are especially involved. One such species that regularly arrives in tiny numbers is the Red-breasted Flycatcher, which breeds in central and northern Europe.

Pied Flycatcher *Ficedula hypoleuca*

This neat summer visitor breeds mainly in deciduous woods in upland valleys, especially in the food-rich sessile oak woods. The Pied Flycatcher nests in holes in trees, and readily uses nest-boxes. The population in some woods has been greatly increased by the erection of such boxes.

Although very obvious while nesting, Pied Flycatchers disappear suddenly after the young have left the nest. Scientists now believe the British population flies straight to the Iberian peninsula, and especially north Portugal, where our birds mix with Pied Flycatchers from other parts of Europe. At this stopping point, they rest and feed, quickly regaining lost fat which gives them the energy to complete their journey and cross the Mediterranean and the Sahara to their winter quarters in west central Africa. In spring, they return by a different route, farther to the east.

Spotted Flycatcher (1)
Slightly smaller than House Sparrow – 14 cm. Very upright when perched. Grey-brown back, whitish underparts and dark streaks on its rather flat head. Juvenile has more streaks on breast. Catches insects in flight and often returns to same perch. Call is a high-pitched 'see' or a sharp 'tsee, tuc, tuc'.
Summer visitor to open woodland throughout Britain and Ireland.

Red-breasted Flycatcher
Size of Blue Tit – 11.5 cm. Smaller than other flycatchers. Dumpy. Grey-brown above, pale underparts. White patches at base of tail and strikingly white undertail-coverts. Often droops wings and flicks tail, frequently cocked up like a Wren's. Female lacks orange throat of male (2). Juvenile like female, but buff spots on wings.
Regular passage migrant on south and east coasts in autumn.

Pied Flycatcher
Smaller than House Sparrow – 13 cm. Plumper than Spotted Flycatcher. Catches insects in the air. Male in spring (3) is black-and-white, but resembles female in autumn. Female (4) and juvenile are brown with white wing-bars. Call is a sharp 'tac', or 'wheet'. Song is two notes repeated with a short trill.
Summer visitor to deciduous woods in Wales, northern and western England and some parts of Scotland. Passes through other areas on migration.

3 Pied Flycatcher ♂

Swallow

4 Pied Flycatcher ♀

Spotted Flycatchers

2 Red-breasted Flycatcher ♂

1 Spotted Flycatcher

Hilary Burn

Bearded Tit *Panurus biarmicus*

The old name of 'Bearded Reedling' was appropriate for this species, which is not closely related to the tits, but to the babblers, a family which is widespread in Africa and Asia.

Once, when there were many more reedbeds than there are today, the Bearded Tit must have been quite common; but, with the draining of so many wetlands and the collecting of eggs and skins in the 19th century, it became a rare species. Cold winters also greatly reduced its numbers and, after the particularly severe winter in 1947, only a few pairs survived in East Anglia. From then on, however, the population started to recover. In 1959, after a good breeding season, many started to erupt from their East Anglian reedbeds and move westwards; this movement occurred again in subsequent autumns, and new colonies were established.

Bearded Tits feed on insects, small snails and seeds, especially the seeds from the common reed *Phragmites*.

Long-tailed Tit *Aegithalos caudatus*

It is the calls of Long-tailed Tits which usually first alert a birdwatcher to the presence of this attractive species. Stand still, and the Long-tailed Tit may come very close.

Long-tailed Tits are only distantly related to the other British tits, from which they differ in a number of ways. For instance, they do not nest in holes, but build a superb dome-shaped nest of moss, spiders' webs and lichens, lined with up to 2,000 feathers.

A large brood of between 8 and 12 young may be reared in the spherical nest, and other Long-tailed Tits may help with the job of feeding the young. These helpers may perhaps have had their own nests destroyed by predators, or they may be inexperienced young birds in their first summer.

Like many other species, Long-tailed Tits die in large numbers in cold winters. During the short midwinter days, they have to spend 90% of the daylight hours feeding; otherwise, they will not survive the long cold nights. In the evenings, little groups huddle together in small roosts so as to conserve heat.

Outside the breeding season, they travel around in flocks, which vary in size between about 5 and 30 or more; sometimes other species such as Goldcrests, Blue Tits, Treecreepers or Chaffinches will mix with these flocks as they rove through woods and hedges in search of food.

Bearded Tit
Larger than House Sparrow – 16.5 cm. Secretive, often flies low with weak, fluttering flight. Tail is very long. Orange-brown body. Male (**1**) has black 'moustache' and grey head. Juvenile (**2**) is like female (**3**), but with dark marks on back. Call is a sharp 'ping, ping.' *Resident in large, dense reedbeds, mainly in southeastern England. Visits smaller reedbeds elsewhere in winter.*

Long-tailed Tit (4)
14 cm. Tiny round body and long tail. Pink, black and white plumage. Juvenile (**5**) has brown on sides of head. Often travels around in small flocks. Call is a high-pitched 'see, see' and a low 'triupp'. *Resident in woods and hedges in most parts of the British Isles.*

Long-tailed Tit

4 Long-tailed Tit

5 Long-tailed Tit *juvenile*

2 Bearded Tit *juvenile*

Blue Tit

Reed Bunting ♂

3 Bearded Tit ♀

1 Bearded Tit ♂

Hilary Burn

Marsh Tit *Parus palustris*

Despite its name, the Marsh Tit tends to be found in drier woods than the closely related, and very similar, Willow Tit. It may sometimes be seen with flocks of other tits, but it seldom travels far from its own territory and pairs generally remain together until one of their rather short lives comes to an end; then, it is quickly replaced by another from a small floating population of unmated Marsh Tits.

Marsh Tits are not common visitors to gardens and are most likely to occur in large gardens with mature trees on the edge of towns. They nest in holes in trees and only rarely use nest-boxes.

Willow Tit *Parus montanus*

The Willow Tit is so similar to the Marsh Tit that it was recognised as a different species only as recently as 1897.

Although Willow Tits may live in the same deciduous woods as Marsh Tits, they are less specialised and may also be found in mixed woods, in conifer plantations and even on farmland with comparatively few trees.

Willow Tits often breed in damp woods, perhaps because that is where there are most rotten tree stumps in which they can excavate their own nest-holes. The excavation is carried out by the female and a new hole is made each year.

Coal Tit *Parus ater*

The Coal Tit, the smallest of the tits, is common in most parts of Britain and will often visit gardens in winter. It is most numerous in coniferous woods and is one of the few species to benefit from the large number of new conifer plantations.

Coal Tits feed mainly on insects. Like the Crested Tits, which also live in coniferous woods, they have a finer bill than those tits which feed mainly in deciduous woods, this adaptation helping them when they probe amongst long conifer needles and cones. When food is plentiful, Coal Tits will often store some of it. An example of this can be seen in gardens when they sometimes hide peanuts in many different places.

Marsh Tit (1)
Size of Blue Tit – 11.5 cm. Small tit with brown back, pale underparts, even paler cheeks, glossy black cap and a small black bib. Juvenile (2) is indistinguishable from juvenile Willow Tit. Call is a loud 'pitchou' and a scolding 'chicka dee-dee-dee'.
Resident in deciduous woods in England, Wales and southern Scotland. Sometimes visits gardens.

Willow Tit (3)
Size of Blue Tit – 11.5 cm. Very similar to Marsh Tit, but with larger, dull black crown, larger black bib, pale wing panel and buff flanks. Call is a buzzing 'eez eez eez' and a loud harsh 'chay' repeated several times.
Resident in both deciduous and coniferous woods in England, Wales and southern Scotland.

Coal Tit (4)
Smaller than Blue Tit – 11 cm. Greenish-grey with pale underparts, a black cap and a white stripe on back of head. Two small wing-bars. Call is a piping 'tsuu'. Song a fast, high-pitched 'teechu, teechu, teechu'.
Resident throughout the British Isles, mainly where there are conifer trees.

Coal Tit
juvenile

Blackcap♂

4 Coal
Tit

1 Marsh Tit

Marsh Tit
juvenile

3 Willow Tits

Hilary Burn

Crested Tit *Parus cristatus*

The old pine forests of the Scottish Highland glens are the home of the Crested Tit in Britain. Once, when the forests were larger, they were probably more widespread, as they still are on the Continent.

Crested Tits usually excavate a nest-hole in the stump of an old pine, but they will also use nest-boxes. They often join roving flocks of other small birds in woods in autumn and winter.

This species is the emblem of the Scottish Ornithologists' Club.

Blue Tit *Parus caeruleus*

Anyone who feeds birds in a garden will be familiar with the Blue Tit. Like many of our garden birds, the Blue Tit is a woodland species and nests in holes; it visits gardens regularly, however, and may be encouraged to stay and nest if a suitable nest-box is provided.

Before and during nesting, the male may be seen feeding the female. This behaviour, known as 'courtship-feeding', is common in some other species as well; it not only helps to keep the pair together, but provides the female with extra food which is vitally important as she will produce more than her own weight of eggs.

Seven to fourteen eggs may be laid, but garden nests often have smaller clutches than those in woodland. Although gardens may be safe places for Blue Tits, there is often a shortage of suitable food. It is easier for them to rear large families in woodland, as a brood of young needs between 600 and 1,000 caterpillars each day.

Great Tit *Parus major*

A Great Tit is more at home on the ground than are the other tits. With its powerful bill, it is able to open nuts and seeds. It regularly visits gardens.

In Britain, Great Tits are largely resident, but may join with other tits in winter. In some years, on the Continent, especially after a good breeding season, tit numbers become large and Great, Blue and Coal Tits move away from their breeding areas; some cross the sea and reach Britain.

Like other members of its family the Great Tit nests in holes. This gives protection to eggs and young, but not against all enemies: weasels raid nests, and Sparrowhawks catch many recently fledged tits.

Crested Tit (1)
Size of Blue Tit – 11.5 cm. Rather plump, with black-and-white crest, brown back, pale underparts and black chin. Call is a distinctive soft, high-pitched purr or trill.
Resident in the mature pine woods of the Scottish Highlands.

Blue Tit (2)
Smaller than Great Tit – 11.5 cm. Very active, often hanging upside down to reach food. Blue crown, white cheeks, yellowish-green back, blue wings and tail and yellow underparts. Juvenile is duller, with yellowish cheeks. Call is 'tsee, tsee, tsee'. Song includes similar notes and also a trill.
Resident throughout the British Isles where there are trees and bushes.

Great Tit (3)
Slightly smaller than House Sparrow – 14 cm. Large tit with black crown, striking white cheeks and black band down the centre of yellow underparts. Male generally has broader black band than female. Young birds are duller and paler. Many different calls including a loud, sharp 'tink, tink'. Song is loud 'tee-chur, tee-chur.'
Resident throughout the British Isles, except in Highland areas and northern islands.

1 Crested Tit

Greenfinches
♂
♀

Great Tit
♂

Blue Tits

Coal Tit

3 Great Tit

2 Blue Tit

Hilary Burn

Nuthatch *Sitta europaea*

These birds nest in holes in trees or, sometimes, in holes in walls or in banks. To stop entry by larger species, the Nuthatch has evolved the habit of plastering mud around the entrance hole until nothing larger than a Nuthatch can get through. They will also use nest-boxes where, of course, the hole is the correct size, but the instinct to plaster is so strong that any cracks are filled with mud and more may be added to the roof, both inside and outside, and to the point where the box joins the tree. Inside, a nest is constructed which comprises large numbers of flakes of bark or dead leaves.

Nuthatches feed on insects or seeds, especially nuts. They will feed on the ground or in trees. On finding a suitable nut, a Nuthatch will usually wedge it in a crevice in the bark and hammer it with its bill until it can get at the contents.

In Britain, a Nuthatch seldom travels far from its breeding territory and this probably explains why it is common in some places, yet absent from others which look just as suitable. Even where numerous, it can be hard to locate until one is familiar with its calls.

Treecreeper *Certhia familiaris*

It is usually difficult to observe a Treecreeper for more than a few seconds because its normal method of feeding is to work its way around a tree trunk, moving upwards all the time, until it reaches the thinner branches, when it flies down to the bottom of another tree and starts to spiral upwards again.

It nests in cavities in tree trunks or behind loose bark. A foundation of small twigs forms the base of the nest and a more delicate cup is built on top. In winter, Treecreepers roost in crevices, but many have discovered the soft bark of the introduced wellingtonia tree, in which they can excavate hollows to fit their tiny bodies.

On the Continent, this species is usually found in coniferous forests in upland areas. In the lower deciduous woods there lives another, closely-related species, the Short-toed Treecreeper *Certhia brachydactyla*, which breeds in the Channel Islands but not in Britain. It is likely that, after the last Ice Age, Treecreepers followed the spread of Scots pine into Britain, but, before the Short-toed could follow the advance of the deciduous trees, the British Isles had become separated from the Continent. Subsequently, our Treecreepers adapted to the food-rich, lowland deciduous woods.

Nuthatch (1)
Size of Great Tit – 14 cm. Climbs with short hops both up and down tree trunks or branches. Short tail and large head, with rather long, stout bill. Blue-grey back and buff underparts. Black stripe through eye. Call is a loud 'tuwit, tuwit'. Song is a repeated 'quee-quee-quee' recalling Kestrel's and Lesser Spotted Woodpecker's songs. *Resident in mature deciduous or mixed woodland in England and Wales. Rare in Scotland.*

Treecreeper (2)
Smaller than Great Tit – 12.5 cm. Mouse-like, as it climbs up tree trunks with jerky movements. Brown, streaked back and whitish underparts. Bill is long and downcurved. Pale wing-bar can sometimes be seen. Call is high-pitched 'tsee, tsee'. Song is 'see, see, see, sissi-see' getting faster towards the end. *Resident in woods throughout the British Isles.*

2 Treecreeper

1 Nuthatches

Wren

Hilary Burn.

Golden Oriole *Oriolus oriolus*

This is a summer migrant to the deciduous forests of central and southern Europe. In spring, a few overshoot their traditional breeding areas and arrive in Britain. Some of these Golden Orioles then stay to nest, and in recent years the number of pairs has increased.

Green Woodpeckers can be mistaken for female and juvenile Golden Orioles as they also have a bounding flight and are similar in colour. Golden Orioles feed on insects, and, in autumn, fruit. They winter mainly in tropical and southern Africa.

Red-backed Shrike *Lanius collurio*

The Red-backed Shrike feeds on insects, including bees, worms, small birds and small mammals. It has evolved the gruesome habit of storing surplus prey by spiking it on thorns or even on the barbs of a barbed wire fence, hence its old, country name of 'Butcher Bird'. Ornithologists call this store its 'larder'.

The Red-backed Shrike has been steadily declining in Britain during the last hundred years. The reason for this decline is not obvious. A gradual change in the climate may have reduced the amount of food available. Heathland, a favourite habitat, is constantly being ploughed up, and egg-collectors regularly prevent the species from breeding at some well-known sites. It may be that while the shrike declines in western Europe it increases in the east; we do not know for certain.

Great Grey Shrike *Lanius excubitor*

A hunting Great Grey Shrike will perch on top of a tree or bush with only its tail moving up and down or from side to side. It resembles a small bird of prey and its habits are similar. Suddenly it will swoop down, grasp its prey and return to a perch. The prey may be eaten at once or stored in the shrike's larder.

Although not common winter visitors, Great Grey Shrikes have regular winter territories and for that reason are quite easy to locate, and their hunting posts are quite predictable.

Great Grey Shrikes feed mainly on small birds, but will also take mammals and insects. They arrive here from October onwards and leave again in early spring for their breeding grounds, which can be anywhere from central France northwards to the Arctic Circle.

Golden Oriole
Smaller than Blackbird – 24 cm. Secretive, spending much time near tops of trees. Male (**1**) has vivid yellow body, black wings and black on tail. Female (**2**) and juvenile are yellowish-green with darker wings. Song is a fluty 'weela-weel'.
Rare summer visitor. A few pairs breed, mainly in southern Britain.

Red-backed Shrike
Smaller than Starling – 17 cm. Often perches on top of bush or fence. Longish tail which is frequently moved up and down or from side to side. Thick bill has hooked tip. Male in summer (**3**) has blue-grey head with black mask and chestnut back. Female (**4**) is duller, and juvenile is like female, but more scaly. Call is a sharp 'chack'.
Rare summer visitor to southern Britain, but others on passage may be seen near the east coast in autumn.

Great Grey Shrike (5)
Smaller than Blackbird – 24 cm. Regularly perches on top of bushes or on wires. Grey upperparts, black mask, pale underparts, and black wings with a white bar. Flight is undulating, and it often hovers.
Winter visitor, mainly to eastern Britain in open country and especially near the coast.

5 Great Grey
Shrike

3 ♂

Red-backed Shrikes

2 ♀

4 ♀

Golden
Orioles

1 ♂

Hilary Burn

Jay *Garrulus glandarius*

The Jay is more often heard than seen. Its harsh calls are often the first sounds one hears on entering a wood and are sure to alarm other woodland species.

Although Jays may be found in most types of woodland, it is in oak woods that they are most typical. They feed on acorns in autumn and regularly store any they cannot eat at once. Not all the acorns stored by Jays are recovered and, as a result, many take root and become young oaks. Thus, Jays are responsible for the regeneration of our oak woods.

Not only acorns are eaten, of course: Jays also feed on insects, as well as other fruits and seeds. In spring, they raid the nests of other species and take eggs and young. It is this feeding behaviour which has made Jays unpopular with gamekeepers, who regularly shoot them.

In spite of persecution, the Jay has managed to colonise new areas, and it appears to be becoming more numerous in towns, where there have been reports of Jays taking food which has been hung up for small birds such as tits.

Magpie *Pica pica*

For years the Magpie has been persecuted by gamekeepers: its habit of feeding on eggs and young of other species resulted in its being shot and trapped in large numbers, especially during the 19th century. The Magpie population has largely recovered during this century and many now breed in towns and cities where they are safer than in game-rearing areas. Magpies may now be more numerous in some towns than on modern farmland where trees and large hedges have been removed, old grassland ploughed up and crops regularly sprayed with insecticides.

The arrival of the Magpie in Ireland can be traced back to a few individuals which crossed the Irish Sea in about 1676, and arrived in Co. Wexford; from then on, the Magpie successfully colonised the whole of Ireland.

Magpies are easy to locate as they are not only large and noisy, but build large, untidy, domed nests made of sticks in tall trees or hedges. Eggs, of course, comprise only a small part of their diet: they also feed on insects, small mammals, carrion, grain and fruit.

Jay (1)
Slightly larger than feral Rock Dove – 34 cm. Secretive, colourful with pinkish-brown body, black-and-white wings with blue patch, and white rump which contrasts with black tail. Wings are rounded, and flight rather jerky. Call is a harsh screech. *Resident in woodland in many parts of the British Isles. Also visits some town parks and gardens.*

Magpie (2)
Size of Rook – 46 cm. Black-and-white with long tail. Wings are rounded and tail often looks wedge-shaped. Call is a harsh 'chack, chack'. *Resident in most of the British Isles except parts of northern Scotland. Usually found where there are small woods or large hedges. Breeds in some towns and often visits large gardens.*

Jay

Magpie

Jay

juvenile

2 Magpies

1 Jay

Hilary Burn.

Chough *Pyrrhocorax pyrrhocorax*

The Chough (pronounced 'chuff') is by far the rarest of our breeding crows and has declined in recent years. Once it regularly nested in Cornwall, and is incorporated into that county's coat of arms, but the last pair nested there in 1960. The reason for its decline is not fully understood: the loss of heathland near coasts, and changes in farming methods and climate, may all have played a part.

Its strangely shaped bill is a valuable tool: it enables the Chough to probe into the ground to find ants, the larvae of other insects and spiders.

Jackdaw *Corvus monedula*

The Jackdaw's liking for bright, shiny objects is well known, and this may even have given it the Latin specific name, *monedula*, meaning 'money-bird', perhaps because of the habit of pet Jackdaws to take coins.

Jackdaws nest in holes in trees or in cliffs, but they also nest in ruined buildings, church towers and chimneys. They usually nest in colonies, and have a complicated system of communication using different attitudes and calls. They are very intelligent and Jackdaws in captivity have learnt quite complicated tricks.

Although they often feed alongside Rooks and other crows, Jackdaws have a shorter bill and take most of their food from on, or near, the surface. They feed largely on insect larvae, but also take young birds, eggs, slugs and worms.

Rook *Corvus frugilegus*

In February, Rooks may be seen returning to their tree-top rookeries and starting to rebuild their nests. In their search for material, they often steal twigs from neighbouring Rooks' nests.

Rooks regularly nest in elm trees, but, since Dutch elm disease swept across Britain, many have been forced to move to other trees. Rookeries in England and Wales average 25 nests, in Northern Ireland the average is 39 nests and in Scotland 79 nests. In 1975, the largest rookery in Britain contained over 2,000 nests.

When Rooks gather food for their young, they store it in an expandable pouch under their bill. They feed by probing into the ground, and take worms, insects and grain. For years, they have been considered a pest and persecuted, but they may be helpful to farmers as many of the insects they eat are harmful to crops.

In winter, Rooks will regularly visit their rookeries, but in the evenings they often join vast communal roosts which include migrant Rooks from the Continent.

Chough (1)
Larger than Jackdaw – 39 cm. Black, with long curved red bill and red legs. Call is a ringing 'chow'. Flight is buoyant. Often performs aerobatics around cliffs.
Resident on rocky coasts of western Britain and Ireland. Sometimes breeds in inland quarries.

Jackdaw (2)
Smaller than Rook – 34 cm. All-black except for grey back to head; pale eye. Often seen in flocks, and mixes with Rooks and Starlings. Flight is rather pigeon-like. Frequently performs aerobatics. Wings look rather pointed, except when soaring. Calls are a sharp 'jac' or a ringing 'kyow'.
Breeds in a variety of habitats, including woods, sea cliffs, quarries and town centres.

Rook
Slightly smaller than Carrion Crow – 46 cm. Adult's (3) all-black plumage looks purple at close range. Face is greyish-white, bill appears long and pointed. Has steep forehead and loose feathers at top of legs. Juvenile (4) is similar to adult, but with dark, feathered face. Similar to Carrion Crow in flight but has longer head, rounded tail, narrower wings and faster wingbeats. Call is a loud 'kaah'.
Feeds on farmland. Breeds in colonies in woods or copses.

Choughs

Rooks

Jackdaw

Carrion
Crow
juvenile

juvenile

4 *juvenile*

1 Choughs

Rooks

2 Jackdaw

3 *adult*

Hilary Burn

Carrion Crow *Corvus corone*

After the Skylark, this is the most widespread breeding species in the British Isles; it is found in many different habitats, from town parks to remote islands.

Although Carrion Crows may sometimes be seen in small flocks, they are more often seen singly or in pairs. They do not nest in colonies like Rooks.

Carrion Crows eat a wide range of food, including insects, worms, grain and fruits. They often feed on dead animals (carrion) and will also catch and kill small animals and birds as well as taking eggs. They have been observed dropping shellfish onto roads and then eating the contents after the shells have been smashed by passing traffic. Carrion Crows have also been seen to break the foil caps on milk bottles in order to get at the cream.

The all-black form of the Carrion Crow is found in western Europe, while the race known as the Hooded Crow lives in northern and eastern Europe and around the Mediterranean. Where the two races meet, they regularly interbreed and hybrids are commonly seen.

Raven *Corvus corax*

The Raven features in legends from Britain, Ireland and many other countries and is often associated with death. Perhaps this grim reputation is not surprising as it is a carrion eater and must have been commonly seen around battlefields and gallows in olden times. As Ravens not only feed on carrion, but also kill mammals and birds and take eggs, they have been persecuted by gamekeepers, but during this century numbers have started to recover.

Ravens usually have four or five different nest-sites within their territory, and they will return to one of these in winter. The eggs are laid as early as February. Nests are generally on cliff ledges, and these are sometimes later used by Peregrines. In some places, Ravens will nest in trees, and some pairs have been seen nesting on pylons.

Where Ravens are plentiful, they will sometimes feed in flocks or gather together in communal roosts in the evenings outside of the breeding season.

Carrion Crow
Slightly larger than Rook – 47 cm. Powerful bill and no white on face. In flight, the tail is square and wings are broad. Flight is strong. Carrion Crows found in most of Britain (**1**) have all-black plumage, but the race found in Ireland and northern and western Scotland, known as the 'Hooded Crow' or 'Hoodie' (**2**), has a grey body. In parts of Scotland, the two races regularly interbreed. Call is a hoarse, croaking 'craah'.
Found throughout the British Isles.

Raven (3)
Larger than Carrion Crow – 64 cm. Largest member of crow family. Has large head, huge bill and shaggy throat feathers. In flight, head projects farther in front of wings than does Carrion Crow's and tail is wedge-shaped. Often performs aerobatics while giving its croaking 'prruk, prruk' call.
Resident in western Britain and Ireland, especially around sea cliffs and in upland areas with crags.

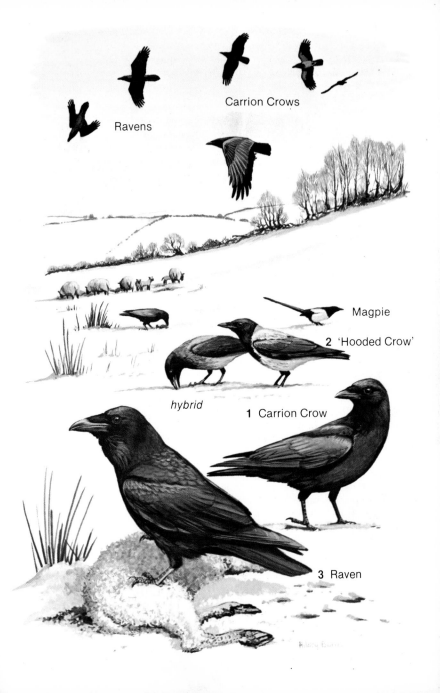

Ravens

Carrion Crows

Magpie

2 'Hooded Crow'

hybrid

1 Carrion Crow

3 Raven

Starling *Sturnus vulgaris*

It is not unusual, in early summer, to come across a pale blue egg lying, unbroken, on a lawn or some other area of short grass. The egg will have been laid there by a Starling which, for a reason that is not understood, is more likely to lay its eggs away from its nest than most other species.

Starlings are often unpopular with people who feed garden birds as, during the winter, they travel around in flocks and gorge themselves on food which was intended for smaller birds. Starlings are, however, rather more interesting than most people realise.

They are superb mimics and their own, typically jumbled songs contain lots of phrases which are copied from other species or other sounds. Curlews, Lapwings, Song Thrushes, Golden Orioles and chickens are all mimicked, as are barking dogs, human whistles and even telephone bells.

Holes in trees, especially old woodpecker holes, are often used as nest-sites by Starlings, but they also use holes in cliffs and walls and nest under the eaves of houses. The nest-holes are often obvious because of the tell-tale white droppings beneath the entrance.

Gardeners should welcome Starlings probing, with their bills slightly open, into a lawn in their search for leatherjackets (the larvae of the cranefly) and other insects. They feed on a variety of other foods, including worms and spiders during the breeding season, and fruit, berries and other vegetable matter at other times of year.

The Starling is a very adaptable and successful species. In past centuries, it was not so widespread as it is now, but in the last hundred years it has become one of our most common birds. In 1890, it was introduced into New York and 65 years later it had colonised most of North America.

For a really exciting spectacle, one has only to locate a local Starling roost at dusk. As early as June, when some Starlings have finished nesting, small flocks may be seen heading for the roost as dusk approaches. The roost may be in woodland, in a reedbed or in a city centre, like the famous roost in Trafalgar Square, London. Later in the year, more Starlings arrive from Europe, and some roosts then number over one million individuals. Before they settle down for the night, they may be seen in large feeding flocks or swooping down to bathe communally before performing some marvellous aerobatics over their roost. Such concentration often attracts birds of prey, such as Sparrowhawks.

Starling

Smaller than Blackbird – 21.5 cm. Rather short tail. Black plumage appears purple or oily green at close quarters. In winter (**1**) many of its feathers have pale tips, giving spangled appearance. Bill is yellow in summer (**2**), horn-coloured in winter. Juvenile (**3**) is brown, with pale throat. Juvenile moulting into adult plumage (**4**) has curious combination of the two plumages. Song is a mixture of scratchy whistles and warbles, often including imitations of other bird calls. Flight is fast and direct, and pointed wings have triangular shape. Except when nesting, is usually seen in flocks and often gathers in vast communal roosts.
Resident throughout the British Isles, except in exposed upland areas.

Starlings

1 *winter*

3 *juvenile*

2 *summer* ♂

4 *juvenile*

2 *summer*

Hilary Burn

House Sparrow *Passer domesticus*

The House Sparrow has benefited enormously from man's activities. Although it probably originated in the steppes of Asia, accidental and intentional introductions by man, to such places as North and South America, South Africa, Australia and New Zealand, have probably made the House Sparrow now the world's most widespread bird species. It is, however, not the most numerous species in the British Isles. It is scarce in remote places where there are no houses to give shelter, and it often depends on man or his animals. Its nest-sites are in any kind of hole, often in a building, but sometimes in trees even in the middle of a wood, or it will build a large, untidy, domed nest in a tree or hedge: House Sparrows often take over House Martins' nests.

Few species have been so successful as the House Sparrow: not only does it use a variety of nest-sites, but it also eats a wide range of foods and quickly exploits new sources: for example, it learnt to copy tits and to hang on peanuts and other food suspended from bird tables. This adaptability explains its success.

House Sparrows have been found nesting in almost every month of the year, but generally they breed between May and August, and often rear three broods. Nests are sometimes close together in loose colonies, and after nesting House Sparrows will flock together. It is at this time that they do most damage, by feeding on grain in agricultural areas.

Tree Sparrow *Passer montanus*

This is the sparrow of woods and fields, rather than towns and gardens. It is unfamiliar to many people, yet it is common in many parts of Britain. It nests in holes in trees, in cliffs and sometimes in buildings. It will also take over Sand Martins' nest-holes.

As Tree Sparrows are smaller than House Sparrows, they can enter nest-boxes designed for Blue Tits. They frequently evict tits which have started to nest. After breeding, Tree Sparrows generally travel around in flocks and often mix with House Sparrows.

Most Tree Sparrows nest in colonies. These colonies may increase or decrease rapidly from year to year for no apparent reason. An example of these rapid changes was seen when the species became extinct in Ireland in 1959 and 1960, yet by 1966 there were at least 50 small colonies again.

Tree Sparrows are common not only in Europe, but also in Asia, where they are usually found around houses like House Sparrows are in Europe, and in some areas are considered to be serious pests.

House Sparrow
14.5 cm. A very familiar species. Male (**1**) has brown, streaked upperparts, grey crown, black throat and whitish cheeks, grey rump and white wing-bar. Female (**2**) is duller, without the bold head markings, but often shows pale stripe over eye. Juvenile (**3**) is similar to female. Call is a loud 'chirrup'.
Common resident. Seldom far from houses or farms.

Tree Sparrow (4)
Smaller than House Sparrow – 14 cm. Similar to male House Sparrow, but has brown crown, smaller black bib, black spot on whitish cheeks and partial white collar. Female is similar to male. Call is 'tek, tek', shorter and sharper than the 'chirrup' of House Sparrow.
Common resident in much of England, Wales and lowland Scotland.

Chaffinch

Corn Bunting

Yellowhammer

Reed
Buntings

4 Tree
Sparrows

juvenile

adult

3 juvenile

1 ♂

House
Sparrows

2 ♀

Hilary Burn

Chaffinch *Fringilla coelebs*

This is one of our most numerous breeding species. Numbers increase in winter when additional Chaffinches, mainly from Norway and Sweden, move south to the Netherlands, cross the sea and arrive in southeast England. On their return journey, they are likely to take a more direct route and fly straight to Scandinavia.

Our resident Chaffinches do not travel far from their breeding territories. Migrants can be recognised because they remain in flocks which usually contain mainly males or mainly females.

The population of Chaffinches appears to have declined since about 1960, possibly as a result of pesticide chemicals used on farmland. It is likely that herbicides used to control weeds may also affect Chaffinch numbers in future as these plants are an important source of food.

Chaffinches are well equipped to feed on a wide variety of food. They have a typical seed-eater's bill which can deal with beech mast (the fruit of the beech tree), grain, and small seeds from common weeds, but is sufficiently pointed to help them catch insects in the breeding season. Insects may be picked off leaves, taken from the ground or caught in the air.

The Chaffinch's song is very variable. It differs noticeably from one part of the country to another, and there are even small differences between the songs of those living in different Scottish glens.

The female, which has the advantage of camouflage, builds the nest and incubates the eggs. The male uses his bright colours in a courtship display. After moulting, the male has buff tips to his bright feathers which make him more like the female, but these tips wear away, and by spring he has bright plumage again.

Brambling *Fringilla montifringilla*

The Brambling takes over from the Chaffinch as the common finch in northern Europe. In northern birch woods it may be the most abundant species, except for the Willow Warbler.

The number of Bramblings visiting the British Isles in winter varies from year to year. The chief food is beech mast; when it is plentiful, there are likely to be more Bramblings around. We get rather fewer Bramblings than some other parts of Europe where huge concentrations may form where mast is abundant. During the winter of 1951–2, it was estimated that 70 million gathered around a single Swiss town when the surrounding beech trees were loaded with mast.

Chaffinch
Slightly larger than House Sparrow – 15 cm. Male (**1**) is colourful, with pinkish breast, two large white wing-bars and white outer tail feathers. Female (**2**) also has white wing-bars and outer tail feathers, but is more uniform brown. Call is loud 'tink' rather like Great Tit's. Song is a loud musical rattle ending in a flourish.
Common breeding species wherever there are trees and bushes. In winter, may be found in many habitats, especially open farmland.

Brambling
Size of House Sparrow – 14.5 cm. Similar to Chaffinch, but with orange sides to breast and bold white rump. Has no white shoulder patch or white in the tail. Male in spring (**3**) has black head. Female (**4**) is duller with grey patch on back of head. Call is a harsh 'tswark'.
Winter visitor to most parts of Britain, but rather scarce in parts of Ireland.

Brambling

Chaffinch

3 Brambling
♂ *spring*

4 ♀

Bramblings

♂ *winter*

2 ♀

Chaffinches

1 ♂

HilaryBurn.

Greenfinch *Carduelis chloris*

These birds often come into gardens in winter, especially if peanuts are on the menu! They are able to hang on most nut-dispensers and often drive away other species.

The Greenfinch's powerful bill is used for breaking open seeds which it finds throughout the year. Young Greenfinches are fed on regurgitated food.

Unlike Chaffinches, Greenfinches nest in loose colonies and defend only small territories around their nests. They will search for food away from the colony in small flocks. The reason for this difference is, presumably, that Chaffinches feed their young on insects which are found throughout their territory: Greenfinches need seeds which may be very plentiful in only a few places.

In winter, some additional Greenfinches arrive here from the Continent and flock sizes increase. Often they join with House Sparrows, Yellowhammers and other species.

In spring, they may be seen singing and displaying over their small territories. They then have a very distinctive, rather slow, deliberate, wavering display-flight, which helps to show off their vivid yellowish wing- and tail-flashes.

Goldfinch *Carduelis carduelis*

Once Goldfinches were common cage-birds, 132,000 being caught in one year near Worthing, Sussex. Fortunately, Goldfinch trapping is now illegal, although it continues in some other parts of Europe.

The favourite food of Goldfinches is thistle seeds, which they can reach with their rather long, slim bills. They are able to cling to swaying stems and will use their feet to grasp their food and draw it towards them.

Many of our Goldfinches migrate to the Continent in autumn, while only a few arrive here from farther north. In spring, Goldfinches may be seen singing and displaying on a branch and as they sing, with wings drooped, they swing from side to side.

Siskin *Carduelis spinus*

The planting of ornamental and commercial conifer trees has helped the Siskin to colonise new areas in Britain and Ireland. It feeds on seeds, especially favouring pines, birch and alder.

Siskins are very agile, and will hang on the thinnest twigs in order to reach their food. This habit of hanging on food has helped them to take advantage of a new source of food: hanging bags of peanuts which have been put out in gardens for tits.

Greenfinch
Size of House Sparrow – 14.5 cm. Large finch with heavy-looking bill. Male (**1**) is brighter green below than above with bright green rump and yellowish-green flashes in wings and tail. Female (**2**) is duller with streaked back, but similar flashes in wings and tail. Juvenile is similar to female, but more streaked. Has twittering flight call. Song is twittering with long drawn-out, nasal 'dzwee'.
Common throughout most of the British Isles and visits gardens in winter.

Goldfinch
Smaller than House Sparrow – 12 cm. Adult (**3**) has red face and a vivid yellow wing-bar on its black wings. Juvenile (**4**) is similar, but without the red face. Flight is bouncing. Call is a tinkling twitter. Musical song is similar to call but longer.
Common resident in most parts of the British Isles except the north of Scotland.

Siskin
Smaller than Greenfinch – 12 cm. Small, streaky, greenish-yellow finch with yellow rump, yellow wing-bar and short, forked tail. Male (**5**) has black cap and bib. Female (**6**) is duller than male without any black on head. Call is a clear 'tsuu' and a hard twittering.
Breeds in conifer woods especially in northern Scotland. Winter visitor to much of southern Britain and Ireland, especially feeding on alder and birch.

Siskin

5 *summer* ♂ *winter* ♂

Siskins

6 ♀

Goldfinches
4 *juvenile*

Siskin *juvenile*

Redpoll

Greenfinch

House
Sparrow

3 Goldfinches

2 ♀

Greenfinches

juvenile

1 ♂

Hilary Burn.

Linnet *Carduelis cannabina*

Once one has learnt the calls of our common finches, one soon discovers that the Linnet is really very common. It is found not only on farmland, where it is among the most numerous breeding species, but also on rough ground near town centres, and it may even nest in large gardens where there are mature shrubs.

Linnets feed mainly on seeds of weeds. They often breed in small colonies and start to nest in April, when seeds become available after the winter. Early nests are usually in evergreen bushes such as gorse, because at that time other shrubs do not have any leaves.

Linnets may join flocks of other seed-eaters when a particular food becomes available: Chaffinches, Bramblings, Greenfinches, Tree Sparrows and buntings may feed with Linnets. In some places food is so plentiful that there is far more than any one bird can eat and so there is no reason why others should not share it. An advantage of feeding in a flock is that since finches feed with their heads down a single bird may not notice a predator, but in a large flock an advancing predator is more likely to be spotted.

Twite *Carduelis flavirostris*

Although Twites are often thought of as 'Mountain Linnets', and they do take over from Linnets in some upland areas, they are also commonly found on windswept cliff-tops, where they search for food on the short cropped turf.

Twites feed, like Linnets, on weed seeds, which are found on farmland. They nest in tall heather, in a hole in a wall or amongst stones on the ground.

Redpoll *Carduelis flammea*

Britain and Ireland are almost at the southern edge of the Redpoll's range and those that breed here are smaller and darker than those farther north.

Redpolls are most common where there are birch trees as their seeds are an important food along with seeds from sallow, alder and many other plants. Some insects are also eaten. Redpolls have colonised many parts of the country in recent years, this spread being helped by the increase in young conifer plantations where they often nest.

Most Redpolls in northern Britain move south for the winter and some cross the Channel to the Continent. Many more leave in years when there is a poor crop of birch seed.

Linnet
Smaller than House Sparrow – 13 cm. Male (**1**) has reddish-brown back, greyish head and red forehead and breast. Female (**2**) lacks any red and is more heavily streaked. Both sexes show white flashes in their wings. Has bouncing flight and twittering flight call. *Found in most parts of the British Isles except for parts of northwest Scotland.*

Twite
Smaller than House Sparrow – 13 cm. Linnet-like, but slimmer, with longer, more forked tail. Brown, with dark streaks; more stripy back, and less white in wings and tail than Linnet. Dark bill in summer, pale yellowish in winter. Male (**3**) has pink rump in summer. Call is a harsh 'cheueet'. Song is similar to Linnet's. *Breeds in upland areas of Scotland and the Pennines, and also on the west coasts of Scotland and Ireland. Winter visitor to the east coast.*

Redpoll
Size of Blue Tit – 11.5 cm. Small and active, often feeding at tops of trees. Dark, streaked back and paler underparts. Male (**4**) has red forehead and breast and black chin. Female (**5**) is similar but the red is duller. Flight is bouncing and usual call is a metallic 'chi-chi-chi-chi'. Song is like call, but with buzzing trills. *Found in most parts of the British Isles, but scarce in the southwest of England.*

Snow Bunting

Twites

Chaffinch

Reed Bunting

3 Twite ♂

Redpoll

Linnets

1 ♂

2 ♀

4 ♂

5 ♀

Redpolls

Hilary Burn.

Crossbill *Loxia curvirostra*

These birds feed on conifer seeds. Their feet are used for holding cones and their strangely-shaped but powerful bill is adapted for extracting the seeds.

Conifer seeds form in cones in autumn, but the cones do not open and release their seeds for between 3 and 22 months, depending on the species of tree. This means there is food available for Crossbills throughout the year. The cone crop, however, varies from year to year and each year Crossbills move until they locate a new supply of cones and will, then, often stay to nest wherever they happen to be.

As well as moving annually, the Crossbill population 'erupts' in some years: perhaps because of the failure of the pine crop, perhaps because of over-population, large numbers leave traditional conifer woods and move far afield, even to areas with no conifers. Some of these Crossbills die, others survive and populate new forests for a time, others return to their traditional areas. In England, many conifer plantations have been temporarily colonised after Crossbill eruptions.

Scottish Crossbill *Loxia scotica*

The remains of the old Caledonian forest of the Scottish Highlands are the home of the Scottish Crossbill, which is now accepted as a true species, not a race, of the Crossbill, as was previously thought.

The Scottish Crossbill has a larger, deeper bill than the Crossbill, and this adaptation helps it to extract seeds from pine cones, whereas the Crossbill feeds mainly on seeds from the softer spruce cones.

Bullfinch *Pyrrhula pyrrhula*

It is unfortunate that this attractive finch is considered a pest in areas where fruit is grown: it is trapped and killed in large numbers. Bullfinches do, however, take many buds – up to 30 per minute – and can spoil a good fruit crop.

Bullfinches are generally seen in pairs and not in flocks. They seldom move far, although in recent years some have shown signs of 'erupting' when their chief winter food, ash seed, is in short supply; it is at such times that most damage is done on fruit farms.

Various seeds are eaten and it is in early spring, when other food is scarce, that they turn to buds. Small snails are also eaten, their shells being broken in the Bullfinch's powerful bill. The young are fed on seeds and insects, which are carried to the nest in two pouches in the floor of the Bullfinch's mouth.

Crossbill
Larger than House Sparrow – 16 cm. Large head, short tail and crossed bill: tips of upper and lower mandibles overlap. Male (**1**) is brick-red (sometimes yellow or orange) with dark wings and tail. Female (**2**) is grey-green with brighter green rump. Juvenile (**3**) is like female, but more streaked. Call is a loud, hard 'chip, chip, chip'. *Breeds in East Anglia, the New Forest, Northumberland, Scotland and a few other places. In some years is found in many other areas as well.*

Scottish Crossbill (4)
Larger than House Sparrow – 16.5 cm. Slightly larger than Crossbill, with larger, heavier bill. Call is loud 'chup, chup, chup.' Otherwise very similar to Crossbill. *Lives in the old pine woods of the Scottish Highlands.*

Bullfinch
Larger than House Sparrow – 15 cm. Plump, neat, with short black bill. Tail, wings and cap are black. Rump is white. Male (**5**) has pinkish-red breast. Female (**6**) has brownish breast. Juvenile (**7**) is similar to female, but lacks black cap. Call is a piping 'dew'. *Resident almost anywhere that there are tangled bushes for nesting.*

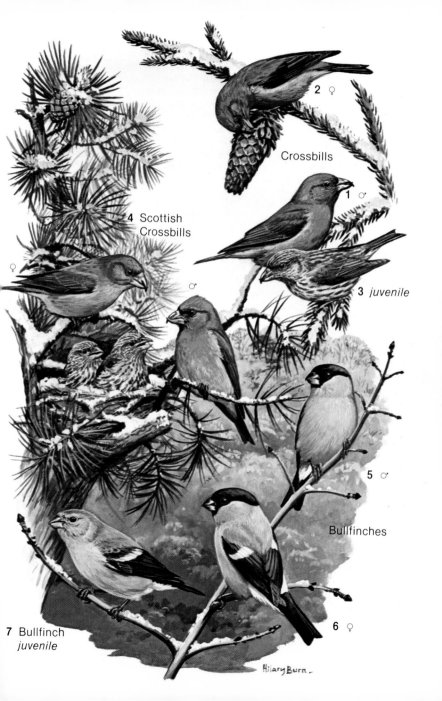

2 ♀

Crossbills

1 ♂

4 Scottish
Crossbills

♀

♂

3 *juvenile*

5 ♂

Bullfinches

7 Bullfinch
juvenile

6 ♀

Hilary Burn

Hawfinch *Coccothraustes coccothraustes*

In summer, Hawfinches feed mainly high up in trees and are very difficult to observe. In winter, they often feed on fallen fruits on the ground, but they are very timid and, again, are difficult to observe. They are most likely to be discovered by hearing their Robin-like calls from high up in tall trees where Robins are unlikely to be.

Some Hawfinches breed in small colonies, while others nest singly. Hawfinches feed on seeds and in summer they also take insects. The massive bill and powerful muscles help the Hawfinch to crack open hard seeds, such as hornbeam, and even cherry stones in order to eat their kernels. The force required to crack a cherry stone is estimated at over 27 kg.

Lapland Bunting *Calcarius lapponicus*

In winter, it is not unusual to come across small flocks of finches and buntings feeding on the seashore or on nearby turf. Sometimes a Lapland Bunting will join one of these flocks, but care is needed in identification, as females, and males in winter, may be confused with Reed Buntings.

Although Lapland Buntings have recently nested for the first time in Scotland, most winter visitors come to us from northern Scandinavia, as their name suggests.

Snow Bunting *Plectrophenax nivalis*

This is the most northerly breeding songbird. It breeds in the far north of Europe, Asia and North America, on both mountains and barren tundra. Food, in the form of insects and seeds, is plentiful, but the summer is short. After breeding, the Snow Bunting moults its feathers and grows new ones before migrating south. The moult is so fast that, in the far north, these birds may become flightless for a short period.

In early spring, the Snow Bunting regularly searches for food in frozen snow, and the ice crystals wear away the feathers around the bill. This species may be unique in having a second partial moult so that new face feathers are grown before the breeding season.

Snow Buntings never move far from snow and ice, but may seek food around houses, like House Sparrows. Others feed on seeds. Travelling in flocks, they feed in their characteristic way: each bird feeds quickly, runs along the ground, then flies to the front of the flock. This 'leap-frogging' means the flock moves forward, in one direction, at about the speed of a man walking quickly.

Hawfinch (1)
Larger than House Sparrow – 18 cm. Largest of our breeding finches, but very shy. Has massive bill and head. Pinkish-brown with black wings, white wing-flashes and white tip to its short tail. Female like male, but duller. Juvenile is less colourful with dark bars on underparts. Call is 'tik' or 'tzik', very similar to call of Robin.
Found in deciduous woods and cherry orchards, mostly in England and a few parts of Wales and Scotland.

Lapland Bunting
Size of Reed Bunting – 15 cm. Male in summer (**2**) has black head and white eye-stripe. Bill is yellow. In winter male resembles female (**3**), which is like female Reed Bunting, but with reddish-brown nape, and two pale wing-bars enclosing rufous patch. Call is a hard 'tick-i-tick', often followed by musical 'teu'.
Has recently nested in Scotland, otherwise a rare, mainly autumn visitor to the east coast.

Snow Bunting
Larger than House Sparrow – 16.5 cm. A stockily-built bunting with white underparts and a lot of white in its wings. Male in summer (**4**) is white with black back and black centre to its tail. Male in winter (**5**) is much browner. Female (**6**) and juvenile show less white than male, but more than any similar species. Call a musical 'teu'.
A few breed in Scotland. Winter visitors elsewhere, especially in north and east.

1 Hawfinches

Reed Bunting

Skylarks **5** Snow Bunting
♂ *winter*

2 ♂

Lapland Buntings

autumn ♀ **3** ♀

6 ♀

Snow Buntings

4 ♂

Hilary Burn

Yellowhammer *Emberiza citrinella*

This is a familiar farmland species. Its distinctive song, and its habit of singing from the top of a bush, or some other obvious perch, make it easy to see in spring and summer when the male is defending his breeding territory. After nesting, however, the territories are abandoned and Yellowhammers may be seen in flocks, often mixed with other buntings, finches and sparrows. In winter, they roost communally in thick bushes or, sometimes, reedbeds.

Yellowhammers feed on seeds, but also eat insects and fruits. Although common on most types of farmland, they are most numerous on highly productive land, especially where there are thick hedges containing a few trees. They are also found on heathland and on the edge of woods.

Cirl Bunting *Emberiza cirlus*

The Cirl Bunting is most numerous in sheltered valleys, and among the vineyards of the Mediterranean region; those found in Britain are on the northern edge of their range.

It is likely that the Cirl Bunting colonised Britain comparatively recently, as the first nest was found in Devon in 1800. It has never been very common, but was, for a time, more widespread than it is now. The species still appears to be declining, perhaps as a result of climatic change, but alterations in farming methods may also be partly responsible. It is now very rare except on the south Devon coast.

Yellowhammer
Larger than House Sparrow – 16.5 cm. Rather slim and long-tailed. Male in spring (**1**) has bright yellow head and breast. Female (**2**) is duller. Both male and female have white outer tail feathers and chestnut rumps. Juvenile resembles dull female and is more streaky. Call is a metallic 'chip'. Song is 'chitti, chitti, chitti, chitti, che-eez', said to sound like 'little bit o' bread and no cheese'. *Found in open country in most parts of Britain and Ireland.*

Cirl Bunting
Slightly smaller than Yellowhammer – 16 cm. Male (**3**) has black throat, black line through eye and greyish-green band across breast, with rest of underparts yellow. Female (**4**) and juvenile are like female Yellowhammer, but rump is brown, not chestnut. Call is a thin 'zit'. Song is a rattle of one note repeated: similar to Lesser Whitethroat's or to the beginning of Yellowhammer's song. *Rather rare. Resident in southern and southwestern England.*

3 Cirl Bunting ♂

1 Yellowhammer ♂

Linnet

4 Cirl Bunting ♀

2 Yellowhammer ♀

Hilary Burn

Reed Bunting *Emberiza schoeniclus*

Many of the wetlands of Britain and Ireland have been drained and most of the species which depend on them have become rarer. The Reed Bunting, however, is an exception. During the last 20 years or so, for a reason that is not really understood, the Reed Bunting has moved into many drier areas such as young conifer plantations and barley fields, as well as continuing to nest in traditional areas near lakes and rivers. Perhaps this change has been forced on the Reed Bunting by a lack of wet sites, the species modifying its requirements to suit the changing environment. Whatever the reason, the Reed Bunting is now firmly established in many places to which it was only a rare visitor a few years ago.

The chief food is seeds, but insects are also eaten in summer. Outside the breeding season, Reed Buntings flock together and often join flocks of other buntings and finches which roam over farmland in their search for food. Recently, Reed Buntings have become more common in gardens and now sometimes visit bird tables in winter.

Corn Bunting *Miliaria calandra*

This large, rather plain bunting is often unnoticed by beginner birdwatchers, yet it is quite common on much of our farmland and is easy to see in spring and summer as it sings from power lines, gate posts or small bushes. Indeed, the Corn Bunting appears to depend on the farmland which man has created.

Corn Buntings spend much of the winter in flocks and may gather in large roosts in the evenings. Males often return to their territories as early as January, but females may remain in their flocks until April or May. Some male Corn Buntings are polygamous, meaning that they have more than one mate in the breeding season.

Nests are often built on the ground in cornfields and this is one farmland species which does not seem to mind the removal of hedges. Its distribution in Britain is puzzlingly patchy: in some places it has recently increased in numbers, while elsewhere it has become scarcer.

Reed Bunting

Slightly larger than House Sparrow – 15 cm. Male (**1**) has black head and white collar, sparrow-like body and white outer tail feathers. Female (**2**) lacks black head markings. Male in autumn is more like female. Call is a loud 'tseep'. Simple song is a very plain 'chink, chink, chink, chittichick'.
Widespread resident in the British Isles. Often found near water, but also in drier places.

Corn Bunting (**3**)

Larger than Yellowhammer – 18 cm. Largest bunting, with large head and heavy bill. Brown with darker streaks, those on breast forming dark patch. Often perches on wires, fence posts and other obvious places. Legs often dangle during short flight away from song post. Call is a short, sharp 'quit'. Song is a short wheezy jangle, said to sound like the rattle of keys.
Resident mainly on arable farmland in many parts of the British Isles. Very local in Ireland and rare in Wales.

3 Corn Bunting

Skylark

Corn Bunting

Reed
Buntings

1 ♂

2 ♀

Hilary Burn

Ornithological Organisations

British Birds is the independent monthly magazine which builds up into a valuable work of reference. It was founded in 1907 and contains articles on identification and bird behaviour as well as reports of unusual species and bird news from Britain and the rest of Europe.

The *British Birds* Rarities Committee is responsible for examining reports of rare birds seen in Britain, and its annual report is published in *British Birds*.

British Birds, Fountains, Park Lane, Blunham, Bedford, MK44 3NJ

The British Trust for Ornithology organises surveys and enquiries which are carried out by amateur ornithologists and administered by a team of professional biologists. The BTO also organises the ringing of birds in Britain. Publications include *BTO News* and the quarterly scientific journal *Bird Study*.

BTO, Beech Grove, Tring, Hertfordshire, HP23 5NR

The Royal Society for the Protection of Birds is the largest voluntary wildlife conservation body in Europe. The RSPB owns important reserves, carries out research, investigates conservation problems and helps to enforce the bird protection laws. There are RSPB members' groups in most parts of the United Kingdom and the Society actively promotes bird study in schools. Members receive the colourful quarterly magazine *Birds*.

RSPB, The Lodge, Sandy, Bedfordshire, SG19 2DL

The Wildfowl Trust manages wildfowl refuges at Slimbridge, Gloucestershire, and at several other centres. The Trust also owns collections of wildfowl for research and education and has encouraged the breeding of some rare species in captivity. The Wildfowl Trust publishes the magazine *Wildfowl World*, and *Wildfowl*, an annual collection of scientific papers.

The Wildfowl Trust, Slimbridge, Gloucester, GL2 7BT

The Young Ornithologists' Club, the junior section of the RSPB, is the largest national organisation for young birdwatchers. The YOC publishes the colourful bi-monthly magazine *Bird Life* which contains articles by experts and by members. The Club runs many projects and competitions, including the annual competition for the Young Ornithologists of the Year. The YOC organises holiday courses in many parts of Britain and Ireland, and runs a network of local members' groups.

YOC, The Lodge, Sandy, Bedfordshire, SG19 2DL

Most of the above organisations will supply a free sample copy of their journals on request.

Index

Page numbers in *italic*
refer to illustrations

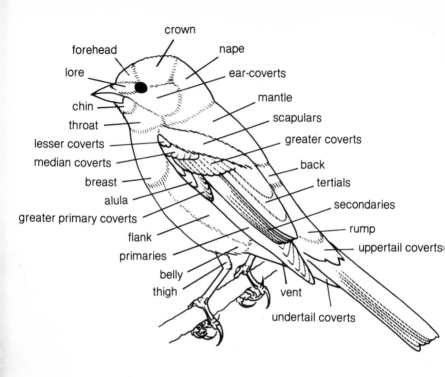

crown

forehead

nape

lore

ear-coverts

chin

mantle

throat

scapulars

lesser coverts

greater coverts

median coverts

back

breast

tertials

alula

secondaries

greater primary coverts

rump

flank

uppertail coverts

primaries

belly

thigh

vent

undertail coverts

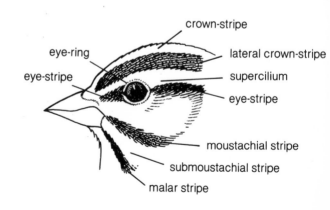

crown-stripe

eye-ring

lateral crown-stripe

eye-stripe

supercilium

eye-stripe

moustachial stripe

submoustachial stripe

malar stripe